Class Tax

Mass Tax

America and Its Underground Economy

PETER S. RUSH

INTRODUCTION

The essential message of the book – rational taxation will produce rational taxpayers is not controversial. In fact, it makes perfect sense to the common man but politicians refuse to listen to the people who pay their salaries. All of the individuals portrayed in the book are composites and any resemblance to a real person is accidental.

I

Everyone is Doing It

"The avoidance of taxes is the only intellectual pursuit that carries any reward"

John Maynard Keynes

Housewives do it; business people do it; senior citizens do it; teenagers do it; teachers do it; preachers do it; cops do it; robbers do it. Nearly every working person in the United States does it at some time during their working life. The Underground Economy is a deep, pervasive and vital segment of the financial well-being of the country. The Treasury Department estimates that the shadow economy contributes nearly $1 trillion to the gross national product.

This money, earned in large and small transactions, in cities, towns and countryside, by rich and poor, involves ordinary people who as intelligent citizens find that the government has no "need to know" everything they are doing. According to the strict interpretation of the tax laws by the IRS, every action from selling puppies to bartering work must be reported. Naturally, without a nation of bookkeepers, few people take the time to report anything but large or steady sources of income.

The legal definition of income, consistently upheld by the courts, includes all gains, not just money, that a person derives from any source except those specifically excluded by the tax code. As the size of the underground economy indicates nearly $2000 for every working person is unreported. Government attempts at forcing the populace into double-entry thinking have failed. As pervasive as the shadow economy is, Americans are voluntary taxpayers when compared to Europeans. Nearly 92 percent of American income is reported and taxes are paid.

But the feeling about that other eight percent, earned by Americans on weekends, in their spare time or on vacation is that it belongs to the individual. Money earned above and beyond the job belongs to the hearty soul who earns it, not to the government. The average person works between 30 and 40 years contributing to the economic health of the country. Money from nearly ten of those years goes solely to the government.

Though not the most heavily taxed people in the world (a dubious distinction), the vast majority of Americans feel that they pay their fair share into government coffers. And when inflation gobbles up buying power and automobiles burn disposable income, Americans in their ingenious way have found enterprises to supplement their income. Included in the underground economy are millions of innocent items from football bets to selling Aunt Lucille's ugly chest of drawers. "House money" my grandmother used to call what she earned from sewing, baking bread and sometimes babysitting. Since the tax man disagrees, the money joins the underground river of cash, pumping initiative and reward into the system.

Though there is a bit of mischief in every heart, the majority of underground money is generated by people who file tax returns each year pay taxes but do not report all their income.

Complicated Internal Revenue rules (no one knows all of the IRS regulations and interpretations) intimidate even accountants. The common taxpayer finds it easier not to report income than to find out where, which form, which records, what tax rate and so on it comes under. At the same time, IRS insistence that all income must be reported is unenforceable. A look at the classified section of any newspaper shows thousands of items which are sold daily with little or no compliance with tax rules. Who can be bothered filling out forms, keeping records or sending in estimated quarterly taxes for those puppies, the old computer, the last garage sale or the azalea plants? Human beings can't be expected to record every transaction in life and they don't.

The catalyst, the medium, the grease of the underground economy is CASH. When the IRS eliminates money so that all transactions between individuals can be electronically monitored by computer, they will have a chance in reducing the evasion. But cash will probably outlive the IRS because, intrinsic in cash, is a security no government can provide. Cash is the protector of the individual. Cash protects the privacy of individual human trade and reinforces confidence in the self. Over $100 billion in cash is in daily circulation in this country with the government constantly printing new bills to replace those worn out by use.

Though credit cards and other plastic money have gained widespread acceptance, the growth of the cash economy has steadily increased since 1776. And while plastic is convenient, it won't make it at the flea market.

The underground economy has no formal structure. It is an amoebic mass of informal networks which responds to individual and market needs and relies on initiative and work for success. It is the quintessence of capitalism and free enterprise. With the adventuring spirit of our ancestors, Americans continue to find constructive and profitable things to do with time. And the shadow economy works because we find it convenient, equitable, lucrative and fun.

A NATION OF RESISTANCE

The American people's experience with taxation has always been a complicated affair. As a country, we recognize the need for taxes to run the government but the form and amount of those taxes has been subject to constant change over the years. Taxes were a root cause of the American Revolution with the original Boston Tea Party a protest against an unpopular tax. However, John Hancock and the major merchants of New England had already established a more effective protest, smuggling of goods so they would have to pay no taxes.

With the development of the country, taxes varied throughout. Mini-revolts from Shay's Rebellion in Massachusetts to the Whiskey rebellion in Pennsylvania to Henry David Thoreau, Proposition 13 in California and the modern Tea Party movement; all were protests about how taxes were collected or how tax money is spent. The link between the ability to tax and the wisdom of how politicians spend the money can generate great debates and start large movements.

And there is the passive-aggressive nature of American's relationship with their government. In the early days of the republic, a simple way to avoid taxes was to move west into the unsettled wilderness. As

3

civilization caught up with the pioneers, they either began paying taxes for the government infrastructure or continued moving to virgin territory. However, that option has run out though there are still pockets that survive in some rural areas of some states. But the passive approach to avoiding the full impact of taxation is done generally without malice rather it is a subconscious decision that enough for the government and more for me.

The debate today which the new Tea Party has brought to legislatures across the country is not only about spending but about taxation. Questions of fairness, transparency, and necessity are being rightly raised and there are no easy answers. But the value of a civilized society in the American tradition is for the individual not the government to decide.

The current climate in America is a recognition that government spends too much. The argument that more taxes are needed is blatantly false because government has never collected more money from the citizens. Rather it is simply a spending problem. And until the American people take the unlimited credit card away from the politicians, the debt will continue to rise. The voice of each individual can be heard when the chorus of truth can drown out the voices of special interests. "If not now, when? If not us, who?" The boldest actions are needed to reset the relationship between the government and the governed. Now is the time to step up and say no more. It is time to bring rationality and accountability back to government. The situation cannot get better without the involvement of all. Avoidance, while expeditious, does not address the underlying problems nor does it contribute to the ultimate cure.

As with every sort of massive human endeavor, the whole is difficult to comprehend. The underground economy in the United States is larger than the gross national product of all but fifteen countries in the world. In other words, this cash economy ranks number fifteen in world economies and has none of the restrictions government regulation puts on visible businesses.

While the dollar size of the shadow economy is staggering, the number of people involved to some degree or another includes practically every American who is trying to put some money away for a rainy day or is just trying to make ends meet. This may rule out a few diligent IRS agents and some unimaginative wage earners with a single salary. But this leaves the rest of the population to dabble at making a buck.

There are three conferences in the league, which I have divided by type of participation in the economy: the "Who me?" conference, the "I forgot" conference, and the "Pro" conference. These divisions are based on the practical consideration of how people are brought into the underground economy. Though many people cross from one conference to another, or play in all three at the same time, the "Who me?" conference accounts for half of all the money and more than half the people.

WHO ME?

The "Who me?" conference encompasses all Americans who under-report their income thus the name "Who me?" Whether by omission, commission or decision, people under-report by not including items that according to strict tax rules must be included. It also includes deliberate methods of under-reporting by omitting items which are difficult for the IRS to turn up without a complete audit. And even then, many things can never be traced (the value of cash transactions).

The dollar value of the "Who me?" is estimated at nearly $500 billion. Since the money is spread over the widest segment of the population and encompasses thousands of items, schemes, occupations and ideas, it is virtually impossible for the IRS to enforce accurate reporting.

The vast majority of these conference players are normal, law-abiding, tax paying citizens. Wages are reported by this group most interest, rent, dividends and stock income is also reported. W-2 forms are the major source of income for this group. Interest from bank deposits are sometimes left out for any number of reasons. But these players pay and feel they are contributing their fair share to the nation's upkeep. Many in this group use the tax laws to gain the most in deductions, benefits, carry-overs and exemptions to reduce their taxable income to a minimum. All done legally.

They are members of the community, often vocal critics of people who do not "uphold" the same high principles the "Who me?" profess. For the most part, "Who me?" do not believe they are doing anything wrong. At least nothing "bad" wrong, rather it is like the ubiquitous white lie, there can be benefit to it.

When confronted with the proposition that they are not reporting all their income to the government, a likely response is "Who me?" And many, in good faith, believe that income simply means their annual salary or total hourly wage. But the government has made it much more difficult than that, and to a large extent, has created the mass participation in the subterranean economy.

When the first income tax was passed in 1913, no effort was made to include every minor or petty deal between people. The purpose of the flat, progressive income tax was to spread the burden of paying for government as equitably as possible among those who could pay. But as government grew, and government programs became more expensive, tax collection became more important. As the tax collection bureaucracy expanded its definitions of income from pressure to collect more each year and the tax courts insisted the taxpayer was guilty until he proved himself innocent, more people were driven outside the strict legal compliance with the law. As the IRS tightened this vise to include barter arrangements between consenting adults as taxable income, it became inevitable that the underground economy would emerge as one of the largest segments of the economy.

Penny-ante transfers of goods and services like selling animals, giving personal instruction, disposing of household goods, accepting gifts and selling handicraft are as old as the country. All of these items have advantages and disadvantages which will be discussed in later chapters. But they are the most common form of under-reporting of income. If my grandmother knew the government wanted twenty-five percent of the money she earned from doing wash or taking in sewing, I doubt if she would have ever started. Few people understand that taxes are supposed to be paid on all these transferred items and women are often the worst offenders.

Waitresses, waiters, bartenders, cabbies, and other people who work for tips are notorious for reporting only part of their income. But corporate employees, especially those with expense accounts have sophisticated methods, with paper documentation, of adding several hundred dollars to their pay each month without paying any taxes on it. Many employers wink at such practices knowing that strict enforcement of expense accounts will only drive away the better employees.

Similarly, the cop who takes a free meal, the professor who tutors, the farmer who sells vegetables, the music teacher who plays for an honorarium have technically violated the law if they do not report these items as income.

With businesses, the process is more complex because, given a good accountant and enough paper receipts most intelligent businesses under-report income as a matter of course. The most obvious are those which deal in cash: bars, restaurants, casinos, retail stores and small shops. This book is not dealing with the largest corporations like Exxon or General Electric because the sophisticated games they play with the IRS using international currency transactions, foreign tax credits and specially designed and executed tax breaks are far beyond the capacity of mere mortals. Suffice it to say that the largest corporations have legal as well as questionable methods of under-reporting and that the government has found it nearly impossible to ferret out these loopholes.

In fact, corporate bribery that emerged as a multi-million dollar pastime during the Watergate years was never detected by the IRS. And the millions in cash, passed by the bluest of the blue chip companies were accepted in corporate circles as just another business expense and routinely hidden among the mountains of receipts and vouchers. The F.B.I. has turned up, with remarkable ease, dozens of elected officials who willingly take cash for favors. And these visible officials are the ones with the most to lose. We cannot speak of these disclosures with any incredulity because the nature of business has always been built around the "favour." Recognizing that Americans, just like any other nationality in the world, are willing if not happy to take cash is only an outcropping of the massive subterranean economy which exists around us.

"I FORGOT" CONFERENCE

While smaller in size, the "I forgot-ers" is as old as the first time the tax collector from the first government came looking for the citizen to pay his tax bill. The non-reporters took to the hills or hid in the forests. What do you think Robin Hood and his merry men were doing living in the forest instead of their homes? They were dodging the taxes of King John, the Sheriff of Nottingham, the local churches, bishoprics, abbeys as well as the special tax levied to ransom King Richard. Avoiding taxes by keeping the government in the dark about your activities is still the safest way to avoid detection. If no one knows you exist, your chances of getting caught are reduced to those incalculable odds of sheer fate. Peasants in Europe during the Middle Ages, as well as peasants today in Asia and Africa, had to hide their earnings from the strong arm tax collectors of the "king's" authority. Being caught for not paying taxes could cost you your life.

The primitive systems of collecting taxes relied on manpower and brute force and the resigned acceptance of the subjugated people. What was paid was done grudgingly. Computers have changed the government - taxpayer relationship since those days.

The machines, running on numbers, easily quantifiable, always correct are slowly trying to process information they receive. Most of the under-reporters are in some danger because of this technological Big Brother.

By not informing the system, the individual reduces the reasons for the machine to look him over. Not informing the system of a second job, hobby, specialty, hustle — whatever it is, is smarter than reporting any part of the income. It works extremely well for those not given to ostentatious displays.

Since sharing within families is difficult, it's easy to understand why everyone hates sharing with the government. Individual risk and trials are taken alone without the help or support of the government. Why should the government get "a piece of the action" if the enterprise is successful and incur no liability if it's a failure? This IRS logic infuriates those who risk much of their own capital and age years in the process of creating profit where there was none.

Adding to the notion that non-reporting of income is the intelligent thing for a prudent person to do is the galactic amounts of dollars that the gargantuan government/military/industrial community consume with no shame. The four and five digit incomes from non-reporting seem civilized when compared to those multi-billion dollar figures. America was founded on the right of all people to work and we work to meet our needs of survival.

In 2009 The Federal Deposit Insurance Corp. (FDIC) reported that 7.7 percent of U.S. households containing at least 17 million adults do not have bank accounts and an estimated 17.9 percent of U.S. households rely on non-bank institutions such as check cashing and money transmitting services.

Some economists estimate that the underground economy in the United States is nearly $1 trillion. In 1998 the Internal Revenue Service officially estimated that the Federal Government alone is not receiving $195 billion per year in revenue due it under the current tax laws almost double the amount the IRS estimated in 1992. These figures are an understandably low estimate.

Non-reported income in the United States according to the official IRS estimates amounts to $345 billion a year. This includes the second job, the income producing hobby, the weekend wheeling-dealing, the low income worker, college kids, and the hearty souls who though earning legal incomes never file returns.

Not filing any return is, by far, the most popular and safest of the "I forgot" conference methods. That is, as long as you are not working for a company or firm which withholds part of your taxes. Then the government has a record which can be checked and documented.

Skilled hands are the most easily concealable asset. If you wear gloves, the IRS man won't see then. Artisans as a class, from the time of weavers and potters, have been able to live the simple life if they chose. Today, carpenters, jewelers, mechanics, painters, web designers and others move freely from job to job, demanding cash payment for certain services. It's an efficient way to service the needs of the economy— both personal and business. And the addition of the mental trades, artists, programmers, architects, copywriters, consultants - the list of saleable skills has increased geometrically.

Those nomads with the gift of gab, the traders and the peddlers have always been difficult to monitor by any form of government. The ability to trade at a profit is a fundamental law of economics. The trader is the equalizer of market forces through his effort and command of information. By knowing who wants what for what price and who has what for what price, he can make the transaction profitable for all three. Of course this role can be expanded as it is in major industries, but the individual hustle is what makes the system work. Cash makes it work better, removing all doubt between the buyer and seller. On any weekend, at thousands of flea markets in every community in the nation, Americans get together to barter and trade. No government, especially a democracy, has any hope of stamping it out.

Naturally, the government isn't stupid about the tricks of individuals and they do have ways to curtail these activities. Many people are audited, some are caught. But these trades and skills, if practiced with some thought are extremely difficult to trace even through diligent police work. The maxim of cash between individuals applies here more than ever.

There are a broad range of incomes which can go un-reported for years. But the drawback to anyone who has ever filed income tax returns is that through some auditing procedures, the government can pick out certain returns after a period of inactivity in the file. And the penalties for non- reporting are stiffer than for under-reporting, depending on the intent.

PRO LEAGUE

This league is primarily, as the name states, for the professional tax dodger who because of other laws, more vigorously enforced, the admission of the income is an admission of the crime. Nevertheless, a segment of the population, primarily male, actively participates on a daily basis.

Drugs and gambling are the most widespread and accepted forms of this cash income. Marijuana accounts for over 70 percent of the drug value, estimated at a $48 billion a year business. The trade in this agricultural commodity is done nationwide, at every level of society, including the children of Presidents, judges, cops and other professionals. Nearly 10 percent of the populace are regular users of pot, primarily for social and personal reasons. The network of pot dealers has grown over the past twenty years into an underground network of efficient and fluid contacts. A simple tax applied to the weed would gather over $10 billion in tax revenues if the government chose to move in that direction. But for now, the cash is directed into the underground economy. Much of this money comes from and supplies the youth market in America. As the college population of the sixties and seventies move into the higher positions of the nation, the pot habit accompanied them. Heroin is a minuscule part of the equation.

Cocaine has become the "champagne" of the middle class. The temptation of pot-powered cash has lured hundreds of thousands of highly educated, sophisticated people. Lawyers, pilots, fishermen and international businessmen of every ilk have profited from the prohibition on pot the way bootleggers did in the roaring 20s. This available cash has led to the wholesale corruption of towns, counties and law enforcement officials. Naturally, no one engaged in this activity declares the income to the IRS. Why? Are you kidding?

As much a crime of volition as smoking pot, gambling is a much older vice and more ubiquitous. Suppressed for centuries by the stern protestant ethic, state governments have in recent years turned a favorable eye to the lottery as a form of voluntary taxation. All but seven states have gone farther in promoting this relatively painless form of taking money in for the state. Yet gambling has always been a popular form of entertainment. Most of the money raised for the American Revolution was obtained through lotteries in the thirteen colonies. Americans, like most people, are willing to put money down on any contest, if the odds are right.

Despite the expansion of government into gambling, the underground betting network is worth nearly $14 billion annually. In the United States, bookmaking accounts for sixty percent of the money, and sporting events are the source of the action. Football sheets can be seen in most bars on any Sunday during the fall. Commentators on national TV give the betting line and they give advice to bettors on the nightly news programs, perfectly aware that the "action" is being wagered illegally. Every now and then, the police bust a "ring," but the sheer number of college and professional sports events defy any possibility of enforcement.

Gambling on sporting events has become so common and accepted in most locales, that mayors of cities often publicly wager something or other on the outcome of a Super Bowl or other contest. It is patriotic to bet on the hometown team.

Though most states have laws prohibiting the wagering of money on sporting events, public sentiment refuses to support the law. Some local governments, like New York, spend millions of dollars in TV, radio and print advertising to encourage citizens to gamble (in New York the city-run Off-track betting parlours only run at loss because of political interference). While organized crime syndicates continue to run their numbers and bookmaking operations, many of these same people are cooperating with governments who have once again discovered this ancient form of tax collection.

With the lessening of moral restrictions and the sexual revolution, the world's oldest profession, is enjoying $20 billion a year in sales. Prostitution is as near as your phone or internet in many cities. While illegal in nearly every state except Nevada (that permits legal brothels), escort services on the internet, massage parlors, and girls on the corner operate with only minor hassles from the authorities. The change in the mores of our society and the liberation of women has contributed to the increase in the freelance and part-time "belle de jour" who work for their own gain without the benefit of a pimp.

There is no pretence at innocence in the Pro league and the government can be extremely harsh with offenders. Organized crime figures have feared the tax man since Al Capone went to Alcatraz for income tax evasion. Yet the physical limitations of enforcement efforts allow thousands of large and small operators to make their fortunes.

SKY'S THE LIMIT

To the millions of immigrants who came and are coming to this country, America is the land of opportunity where the streets are paved with gold. While not literally true, Americans have nearly unfettered freedom to work for that pot of gold. The perception of the possibility draws incentive from the individual, adding value to the goods and services and, at the same time brings the creative talents and strengths to the surface.

Horatio Alger recognized the dream of "rags to riches" 160 years ago and for millions that dream has consistently come true. Our self-made character is fundamental to the existence and prosperity of the underground economy, as well as the rest of the nation. As economists consistently make wrong assessments as to the will of the nation to be prosperous, IRS officials want more police power, more money and bigger computers to stamp out the fifteenth largest economy in the world.

Thousands of the brightest and most ambitious people of the world flock to the United States of America, to feel the vibrancy of a country, motivated for the most part by nonviolent self-interest. As long as people are producing and making money, the system will prosper. The underground economy has produced millionaires in the country who often continue successfully into legitimate business. It is the capital market for the small individual who trades skill, determination and thought for money.

As in any other human enterprise, some people succeed while others fail. Yet failure in the underground economy is of will rather than ways to achieve that desired success. Millions of people are involved in making a better life for themselves and family by using their talents and skills to their maximum economic potential.

With the vanishing of the American frontier, historians declared an end to the individual heroism of the country. Our genius for invention, drawn from the idiosyncratic population, feeds both the above and below ground economic streams of innovation and success. American wealth is not static, not enshrined in the hands of a few, but continually washes through our hands.

No one can avoid taxes. From birth to death, there are hundreds of ways the government extracts money from the citizenry. In the underground economy, people avoid the taxes they can and pay what they must. There isn't any argument about the necessity for taxes only about the amount and type.

This shadow economy has grown in recent years in direct relation to the increase in government rules, regulations and unemployment. By putting the taxpayer on the defensive, by assuming the taxpayer is guilty until proven innocent, the government has challenged the individual to "get away" with evasion. Since the complexity of the laws is beyond the grasp of all but a few specialists, we allow ignorance (or feigned ignorance) to be our bulwark.

While the existence of the underground economy continues to be a source of irritation to the Internal Revenue Service, the elasticity which it builds into our national economic landscape provides constructive, productive channels for our national desire to make a dollar. And there has never been much shame in getting rich.

Every type of personality, with any kind of skill, can find ways to earn cash in the underground economy. A second income based on hobbies, crafts, and awareness is there for the taking. Individualism and talent are important but not critical factors in your success. Organization and the will to achieve work equally as well.

Looking for the "better way" has been the occupation of mankind since questions of basic survival have been answered. In our democracy, economic freedom is the fundamental strength of our way of life. There is no way, short of a Big Brother rule, that the government can hope to police or halt the exercise of this basic economic freedom.

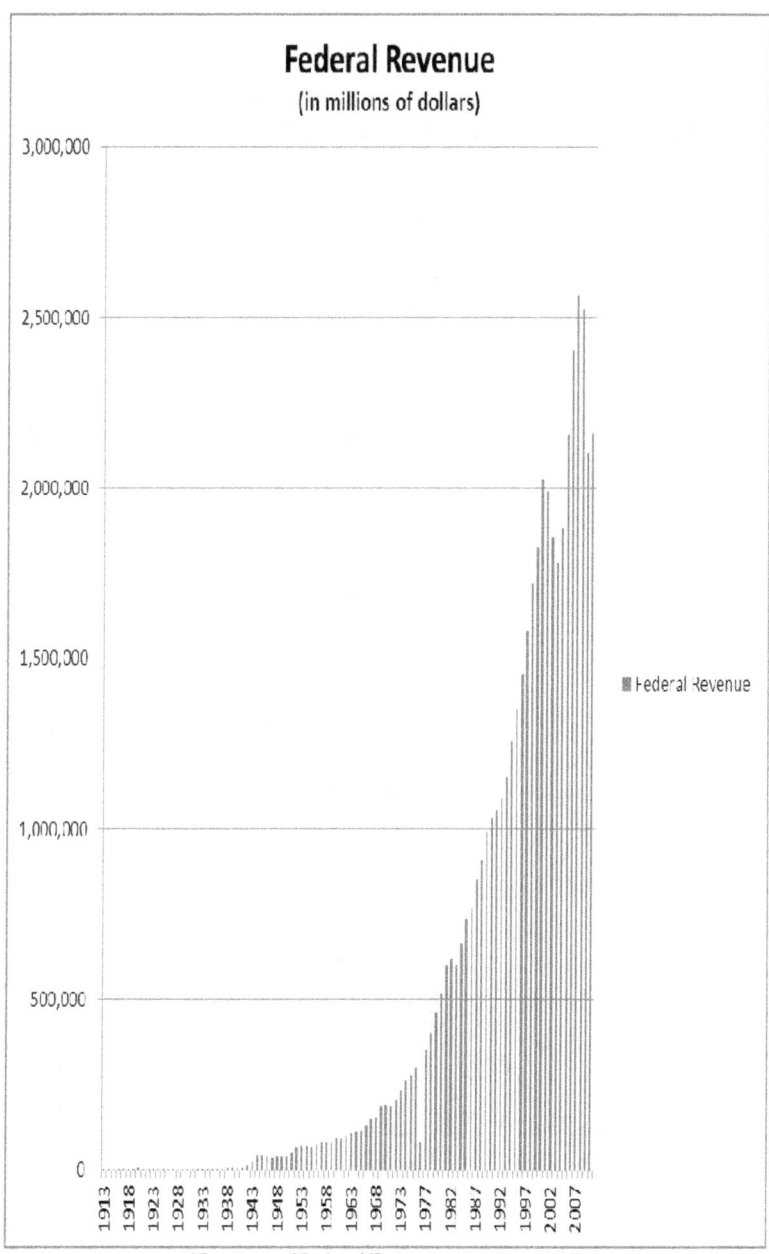

Figure 1 - Federal Revenue 1913 - 2010

II

A SHORT HISTORY OF TAXATION

"I believe the income tax does more than any other tax to demoralize and corrupt the people. It tends to make us a nation of liars. It is a tax upon the income of honest men and an exemption of the income of rascals."

Gladstone

No one loves to pay taxes. From the time the first tribal leader demanded a share of his kin's produce as a price for protection, tax systems have been inequitable and contradictory. But the personal income tax, converted to a mass tax in 1941, has expanded the government's ability to raise revenue beyond the wildest dreams of any king. The income tax, once hailed as the way to prevent the concentration of wealth in a few hands, has become an albatross around the neck of the common man.

Yet the passage of the 16th Amendment permitting the collection of income taxes was generally hailed as a progressive step when it wasn't otherwise ignored by the press. No one imagined in 1913 that the income tax would become the monster of American life. The first income tax applied to less than 1 percent of the entire population. Today, 95 percent of the adult population is required to file. The income tax created the money flow for the government to grow from a very modest beginning to a federal budget of $1.3 trillion plus the cost of state and local governments. How did we get into this mess? A brief look at the history of taxation and its politics in America reveals the human hand.

REVOLUTIONARY AMERICA

The American Revolution was fought for a myriad of reasons but taxation was the bread and butter issue. "Taxation without representation is tyranny" was the battle cry and the words continue to reverberate today. Our forefathers who were protesting such impositions as a stamp act and import duties on items such as tea

16

would be confounded by the broad taxes on everything in today's society.

In America during British rule, the government assumed limited responsibility, consisting of defense and the protection of trade. No money was spent on social welfare and little on public improvements. Taxes collected by the colonies were light and varied by regions. The South controlled by large landowners disliked taxes on land. There, taxes were placed on imports and exports. The middle colonies levied both a property tax and the head tax, so much for each adult male regardless of his income. New England used a general real-estate tax, an excise tax on luxury goods and a "faculty tax" on the gains of the arts, trades, professions and handicrafts.

When the Constitution was drawn, the sovereign states jealously withheld essential powers from Congress including the power to levy direct taxes. During the early 19th Century, the federal government was financed chiefly by tariff duties, sale of public lands and various temporary excises and internal taxes. The revenue of the Treasury fluctuated between surpluses and deficits. When the money was available, Congress, like most humans, spent it.

In 1861, the Civil War changed forever the political concepts of taxation. The first income tax of 3 percent on all incomes above $800 was levied as a War Tax. The law authorized the Secretary of the Treasury to hire employees to detect fraud and provided for the establishment of a permanent tax collecting agency, the Bureau of Internal Revenue. The Civil War tax gatherers were paid a commission on the dollars they collected which assured their interest in the bottom line figures.

After the war ended, patriotism subsided and support for the income tax quickly disappeared. Public pressure by well-to-do Northerners quickly became a political liability for the Grant administration. In 1872, ten years after its adoption, the income tax was repealed. The government again turned to the tariff and taxes on alcohol and tobacco to run the affairs of state.

But the politics of the day pitted Congressmen from farm states who favored railroad regulation, cheap money, free silver and income and inheritance taxes against the industrialists of the Northern states who wanted sound money, taxes on consumption (tariffs) and the gold standard. In 1893, the farmer's coalition carried the day and a new income tax was added to the tariff bill. Arguments against the tax then are still heard today. It is socialism. It penalizes thrift. It is a tax of tyrants. It encourages dishonesty and perjury, bringing on spies and informers. Two years later, the Supreme Court ruled the income tax was unconstitutional.

During the next fifteen years, the pressure for an income tax continued to mount. The working public at large, enraged at the affluence of the "robber barons" like Rockefeller, Astor, Carnegie and the sweat shop conditions of the newer immigrants wanted a tax on the rich. It was only fair, the theory went that the rich should pay a greater share for government. This class argument can still be heard today.

With budget deficits mounting because of the more costly navy and government services, even the most conservative Republicans were looking for a better means to raise money. The tariff system was cumbersome and unreliable. Public lands had mostly been sold. Increased American involvement in the Philippines, Panama Canal and Hawaii had brought the United States into competition with the world powers. In 1909, Congress passed a corporation tax and sponsored a joint resolution which submitted a constitutional amendment to the states providing for direct taxation. The objective was to tax the *rich* – to make them pay *Their Fair Share.*

THE SIXTEETH AMENDMENT

On February 3, 1913, Wyoming became the thirty-sixth state to ratify the Sixteenth Amendment which provided the three fourths of the states necessary to ratify the amendment. The income tax became a fixture in American life. No one dreamed that the income tax would become the all-inclusive, complicated mess it is today.

In 1914, the first taxes were collected as 357,598 people filed, less than one-half of one percent of the population. The tax rate was meager by today's standards. The first $3000 which would equal $65,500 in 2010, ($4000 for a married couple = $86,500 in 2010) was exempt from taxes. After that, the taxpayer was assessed 1percent on the first $20,000 up to a maximum of 6 percent for those with incomes over $500,000 =$10 million in 2010. There were exemptions for business expenses and capital losses but very few compared to the boggling number today. (See figure 2 below)

Form 1040.

INCOME TAX.

THE PENALTY
FOR FAILURE TO HAVE THIS RETURN IN
THE HANDS OF THE COLLECTOR OF
INTERNAL REVENUE ON OR BEFORE
MARCH 1 IS $20 TO $1,000.
(SEE INSTRUCTIONS ON PAGE 4.)

UNITED STATES INTERNAL REVENUE.

RETURN OF ANNUAL NET INCOME OF INDIVIDUALS.

(As provided by Act of Congress, approved October 3, 1913.)

RETURN OF NET INCOME RECEIVED OR ACCRUED DURING THE YEAR ENDED DECEMBER 31, 191 ....

(FOR THE YEAR 1913, FROM MARCH 1, TO DECEMBER 31.)

Filed by (or for) .... of ....
(Full name of individual.) (Street and No.)

in the City, Town, or Post Office of .... State of ....
(Fill in pages 2 and 3 before making entries below.)

1. GROSS INCOME (see page 2, line 12)	$	
2. GENERAL DEDUCTIONS (see page 3, line 7)	$	
3. NET INCOME	$	

Deductions and exemptions allowed in computing income subject to the normal tax of 1 per cent.

4. Dividends and net earnings received or accrued, of corporations, etc., subject to like tax. (See page 2, line 11) . .	$	
5. Amount of income on which the normal tax has been deducted and withheld at the source. (See page 2, line 9, column A)		
6. Specific exemption of $3,000 or $4,000, as the case may be. (See Instructions 3 and 19)		
Total deductions and exemptions. (Items 4, 5, and 6)	$	
7. TAXABLE INCOME on which the normal tax of 1 per cent is to be calculated. (See Instruction 3) .	$	

8. When the net income shown above on line 3 exceeds $20,000, the additional tax thereon must be calculated as per schedule below:

				INCOME.	TAX.
1	per cent on amount over $20,000 and not exceeding $50,000 . .	$		$	
2	"	"	50,000 " " 75,000 .			
3	"	"	75,000 " " 100,000 .			
4	"	"	100,000 " " 250,000 .			
5	"	"	250,000 " " 500,000 .			
6	"	"	500,000			
		Total additional or super tax	$		
		Total normal tax (1 per cent of amount entered on line 7) . .	$		
		Total tax liability	$		

Figure 2 - Page 1 of 1913 Income Tax Form

GROSS INCOME.

This statement must show in the proper spaces the entire amount of gains, profits, and income received by or accrued to the individual from all sources during the year specified on page 1.

DESCRIPTION OF INCOME.	A. Amount of income on which tax has been deducted and withheld at the source.	B. Amount of income on which tax has NOT been deducted and withheld at the source
1. Total amount derived from salaries, wages, or compensation for personal service of whatever kind and in whatever form paid	$	$
2. Total amount derived from professions, vocations, businesses, trade, commerce, or sales or dealings in property, whether real or personal, growing out of the ownership or use of interest in real or personal property, including bonds, stocks, etc.		
3. Total amount derived from rents and from interest on notes, mortgages, and securities (other than reported on lines 5 and 6)		
4. Total amount of gains and profits derived from partnership business, whether the same be divided and distributed or not		
5. Total amount of fixed and determinable annual gains, profits, and income derived from interest upon bonds and mortgages or deeds of trust, or other similar obligations of corporations, joint-stock companies or associations, and insurance companies, whether payable annually or at shorter or longer periods		
6. Total amount of income derived from coupons, checks, or bills of exchange for or in payment of interest upon bonds issued in *foreign countries* and upon *foreign mortgages* or like obligations (not payable in the United States), and also from coupons, checks, or bills of exchange for or in payment of any dividends upon the stock or interest upon the obligations of foreign corporations, associations, and insurance companies engaged in business in foreign countries		
7. Total amount of income received from fiduciaries . . .		
8. Total amount of income derived from any source whatever, not specified or entered elsewhere on this page		
9. TOTALS		
NOTES.—Enter total of Column A on line 5 of first page.		
10. AGGREGATE TOTALS OF COLUMNS A AND B	$	
11. Total amount of income derived from dividends on the stock or from the net earnings of corporations, joint-stock companies, associations, or insurance companies subject to like tax (To be entered on line 4 of first page.)	$	
12. TOTAL "**Gross Income**" (to be entered on line 1 of first page)	$	

GENERAL DEDUCTIONS.

1. The amount of necessary expenses actually paid in carrying on business, but not including business expenses of partnerships, and not including personal, living, or family expenses . $

2. All interest paid within the year on personal indebtedness of taxpayer . . . .

3. All national, State, county, school, and municipal taxes paid within the year (not including those assessed against local benefits) . . . .

4. Losses actually sustained during the year incurred in trade or arising from fires, storms, or shipwreck, and not compensated for by insurance or otherwise . . . .

5. Debts due which have been actually ascertained to be worthless and which have been charged off within the year . . . .

6. Amount representing a reasonable allowance for the exhaustion, wear, and tear of property arising out of its use or employment in the business, not to exceed, in the case of mines, 5 per cent of the gross value at the mine of the output for the year for which the computation is made, but no deduction shall be made for any amount of expense of restoring property or making good the exhaustion thereof, for which an allowance is or has been made . . .

7. Total "GENERAL DEDUCTIONS" (to be entered on line 2 of first page) . . . .

AFFIDAVIT TO BE EXECUTED BY INDIVIDUAL MAKING HIS OWN RETURN.

I solemnly swear (or affirm) that the foregoing return, to the best of my knowledge and belief, contains a true and complete statement of all gains, profits, and income received by or accrued to me during the year for which the return is made, and that I am entitled to all the deductions and exemptions entered or claimed therein, under the Federal Income-tax Law of October 3, 1913.

Sworn to and subscribed before me this ....

day of .... , 191

(Signature of individual.)

SEAL OF
OFFICER
TAKING
AFFIDAVIT.

(Official capacity.)

AFFIDAVIT TO BE EXECUTED BY DULY AUTHORIZED AGENT MAKING RETURN FOR INDIVIDUAL.

I solemnly swear (or affirm) that I have sufficient knowledge of the affairs and property of .... to enable me to make a full and complete return thereof, and that the foregoing return, to the best of my knowledge and belief, contains a true and complete statement of all gains, profits, and income received by or accrued to said individual during the year for which the return is made, and that the said individual is entitled, under the Federal Income-tax Law of October 3, 1913, to all the deductions and exemptions entered or claimed therein.

Sworn to and subscribed before me this ....

day of .... , 191

(Signature of agent.)

ADDRESS
IN FULL

SEAL OF
OFFICER
TAKING
AFFIDAVIT.

(Official capacity.)

[SEE INSTRUCTIONS ON BACK OF THIS PAGE.]

INSTRUCTIONS.

1. This return shall be made by every citizen of the United States, whether residing at home or abroad, and by every person residing in the United States, though not a citizen thereof, having a *net income* of $3,000 or over for the taxable year, and *also by every nonresident alien* deriving income from property owned and business, trade, or profession carried on in *the United States* by him.

2. When an individual by reason of minority, sickness or other disability, or absence from the United States, is unable to make his own return, it may be made for him by his *duly authorized* representative.

3. The *normal tax* of 1 per cent shall be assessed on the total net income less the specific exemption of $3,000 or $4,000 as the case may be. (For the year 1913, the specific exemption allowable is $2,500 or $3,333.33, as the case may be.) If, however, the normal tax has been deducted and withheld on any part of the income at the source, or if any part of the income is received as dividends upon the stock or from the net earnings of any corporation, etc., which is taxable upon its net income, such income shall be deducted from the individual's total *net income* for the purpose of calculating the amount of income on which the individual is liable for the normal tax of 1 per cent by virtue of this return. (See page 1, line 7.)

4. The *additional or super tax* shall be calculated as stated on page 1.

5. This return shall be filed with the Collector of Internal Revenue for the district in which the individual resides if he has no other place of business, otherwise in the district in which he has his *principal place of business*; or in case the person resides in a foreign country, then with the collector for the district in which his principal business is carried on in the United States.

6. This return must be filed on or before the first day of March succeeding the close of the calendar year for which return is made.

7. The *penalty for failure to file the return within the time specified by law* is $20 to $1,000. In case of refusal or neglect to render the return within the required time (except in cases of sickness or absence), 50 per cent shall be added to amount of tax assessed. In case of *false or fraudulent return*, 100 per cent shall be added to such tax, and any person required by law to make, render, sign, or verify any return who makes any false or fraudulent return or statement with intent to defeat or evade the assessment required by this section to be made shall be guilty of a misdemeanor, and shall be fined not exceeding $2,000 or be imprisoned not exceeding one year, or both, at the discretion of the court, with the costs of prosecution.

8. When the return is not filed within the required time by reason of sickness or absence of the individual, an extension of time, not exceeding 30 days from March 1, within which to file such return, *may be granted by the collector, provided an application therefor is made by the individual within the period for which such extension is desired.*

9. This return properly filled out must be made under oath or affirmation. Affidavits may be made before any officer *authorized by law* to administer oaths. If before a justice of the peace or magistrate, not using a seal, a *certificate of the clerk of the court as to the authority* of such officer to administer oaths should be *attached to the return.*

10. Expense for medical attendance, store accounts, family supplies, wages of domestic servants, cost of board, room, or house rent for family or personal use, *are not expenses that can be deducted from gross income.* In case an individual owns his own residence he can not deduct the estimated value of his rent, neither shall he be required to include such estimated rental of his home as income.

11. The farmer, in computing the net income from his farm for his annual return, shall include all moneys received for produce and animals sold, and for the wool and hides of animals slaughtered, provided such wool and hides are sold, and he shall deduct therefrom the sums actually paid as purchase money for the animals sold or slaughtered during the year.

When animals were raised by the owner and are sold or slaughtered he shall not deduct their value as expenses or loss. He may deduct the amount of money actually paid as expense for producing any farm products, live stock, etc. In deducting expenses for repairs on farm property the amount deducted must not exceed the amount actually expended for such repairs during the year for which the return is made. (See page 3, item 6.) The cost of replacing tools or machinery is a deductible expense to the extent that the cost of the new articles does not exceed the value of the old.

12. In calculating losses, only such losses as shall have been actually sustained and the amount of which has been definitely ascertained during the year covered by the return can be deducted.

13. Persons receiving fees or emoluments for professional or other services, as in the case of physicians or lawyers, should include all actual receipts for services rendered in the year for which return is made, together with all unpaid accounts, charges for services, or contingent income due for that year, if good and collectible.

14. Debts which were contracted during the year for which return is made, but found in said year to be worthless, may be deducted from gross income for said year, but such debts can not be regarded as worthless until after legal proceedings to recover the same have proved fruitless, or it clearly appears that the debtor is insolvent. If debts contracted prior to the year for which return is made were included as income in return for any prior year at which said debts were contracted, and such debts shall subsequently prove to be worthless, they may be deducted under the head of losses in the return for the year in which such debts were charged off as worthless.

15. Amounts due or accrued to the individual members of a partnership from the net earnings of the partnership, whether apportioned and distributed or not, shall be included in the annual return of the individual.

16. United States pensions shall be included as income.

17. Estimated advance in value of real estate is not required to be reported as income, unless the increased value is taken up on the books of the individual as an increase of assets.

18. Costs of suits and other legal proceedings arising from ordinary business may be treated as an expense of such business, and may be deducted from gross income for the year in which such costs were paid.

19. An unmarried individual or a married individual not living with wife or husband shall be allowed an exemption of $3,000. When husband and wife live together they shall be allowed jointly a total exemption of only $4,000 on their aggregate income. They may make a joint return, both subscribing thereto, or if they have separate incomes, they may make separate returns; but in no case shall they jointly claim more than $4,000 exemption on their aggregate income.

20. In computing net income there shall be excluded the compensation of all officers and employees of a State or any political subdivision thereof, except when such compensation is paid by the United States Government.

Figure 3 - The entire tax instructions - 1913

The generous exemption, which today would be worth $65,500 to $86,500 was designed to allow the majority of the population to live a comfortable life before the heavy obligation of supporting the government was imposed. Our present politicians work on the theory that the government should collect as much money as possible from every citizen, including the poor, and then redistribute the income through costly government programs.

The small segment of the population who were required to file taxes accounts for the limited reaction to the first income tax but the possibilities of direct taxation was not lost in Washington. Since the passage of the Income Tax, it has been a yearly *political* football between the Democrats and Republicans. While taxes have steadily increased since the early years, politicians of every ilk speak in favor of tax cuts. The duplicity of political promises has made the public skeptical toward any hope of a real reduction in the tax burden. One section of the 1921 revenue bill required that the name of the taxpayer and the amount he paid in taxes be published in the local newspaper. Needless to say, the prurient interest of the public could not match the outrage of the taxpayer to having his most private affairs hung like so much dirty underwear in full public view. This segment of the income tax, which was repealed in 1926 to be re-imposed in 1934 to finally be permanently repealed two years later, was a further incentive not to pay taxes. The reason the publicity requirement was repealed is simple - no one complied.

The quiet acceptance of the income tax was accelerated by world events, namely the First World War which was already underway in Europe when the tax became law. In 1915, the government launched a Preparedness Campaign stirring patriotic sentiment to a frenzy. A year later with gasoline prices doubling from $0.11 to $0.23 overnight, a new War Revenue Act was adopted by Congress taxing some income as high as 67 percent while lowering the exemptions.

During the next two years of war, the federal government conducted a massive propaganda campaign supporting tax collection as the only way to save the country and the world. Churches preached sermons, schools taught patriotism, and utilities printed handbills supporting tax collection. By the end of 1918, the revenue structure of the United States government was irreversibly addicted to the direct income tax, the greatest source of revenue any government had ever found. And the massive voluntary compliance by the patriotic public created a bucolic air of an endless money spigot.

With the end of the war and the passage of Prohibition a different mood settled on the country. Disillusionment with the "War to End All Wars" weariness and a sense of frustration over the loss of the pleasures of liquor changed the complexion of the public. The loss of liquor revenues, the third largest source of income, placed a greater burden on the general revenue tax. A general "tax phobia" settled over the skeptical public, who, while paying taxes, did so more reluctantly and with little accuracy. This led to a trimming of the tax rates.

But with the appearance of a huge deficit during the early years of the Depression, the rates were again raised. The tax base was broadened and the exemptions were lowered. The acceptance of Keynesian economic theory permitted Roosevelt to spend in the deficit to "prime the pump of private economy."

By 1937, tax avoidance and evasion were rampant. Early in the century, J.P. Morgan Jr. expressed it succinctly when he said that taxation was a legal question not a moral one. "Congress should know how to levy taxes and if it doesn't know how to collect them, then a man is a fool to pay them."

An army of lawyers and accountants were hired by the wealthy to pour over the tax laws, finding ways to circumvent the always vague statutes. "Loopholes" as they were later politically called were invented. Phony corporations, incorporation of private fortunes, tax-exempt charitable foundations and the like, permitted the wealthy to protect their wealth from the government.

To combat the growing tax rebellion, the Bureau of Internal Revenue concentrated on big name cases of tax evasion in order to instill fear and prod compliance. Al Capone, George M. Cohan, Gloria Swanson, John Barrymore and Joe Louis were valuable to the tax gatherers as "showcases" of the possible penalties for not complying with the law. This spurt in enforcement was aimed at sagging compliance during the economic hard times of the Depression.

In 1939 the income tax was still as much a privilege of the rich as Newport in the summer or trans-Atlantic luxury cruises. Only four million Americans were liable for any taxes that year, less than one percent of the population. But as the democratization of America continued, the "privilege of paying" taxes were passed onto the entire population.

WORLD WAR II AND THE MASSIVE TAX

The total mobilization of American society to fight the industrial power of Germany and Japan changed the relationship of Americans with their government. Government became the focus of national attention for the right thing to do Washington hired "experts" to run the country. As with any war, military hardware must be paid for with money, the people's money. Taxes had to be raised to pay for the very expensive projects of the government.

In 1941, a tax bill lowered the exemption to include millions of citizens. By 1945, 49,865,000 citizens or 36 percent of the population were paying income taxes. Using the "new" techniques of mass media propaganda to urge the acceptance of these necessary "war taxes", radio messages, songs, billboards and advertisements played upon the patriotic sentiments of all Americans. Give your money to the government, tomorrow you can have that refrigerator. Willing Americans heeded the calls of their leaders.

In 1942, without the slightest ripple of opposition, the now ubiquitous "withholding" provision of the income tax became law. The citizen began paying the government weekly or monthly (depending on the pay period) instead of once a year. American business, as the employer, took over the enforcement of this tax collection by deducting the taxes before rendering the pay check. Today, in some cities, that deduction is nearly forty percent of the salary. The incumbent paperwork and new bureaucracies this created were dwarfed by the results of this marvelously simple idea.

Tax revenues poured into the Treasury, and the government learned that it could tax its people (voluntarily) much more heavily than was previously thought possible. Federal revenues grew from an average

26

of $4 billion per year in 1939 to $26 billion a year in 1946. All the money was voluntarily given to Washington to spend on the defense of the country. But the end of the war did not mean the end of the taxes.

Winning the war gave new status to government and created the image that government could do anything. Those in power, in the post war afterglow, were shocked at the sudden reversals of the economy in 1946 after controls on prices, wages and other rationed items were released to market forces.

High inflation, unemployment, millions of militant veterans looking for a better life kept Keynesian economics at the forefront in Washington. Taxes were not reduced and government spending, though slowed in the years directly following the war, began climbing throughout the fifties. The Korean War cut short any hope of reduced taxes, and the income tax remained a mass tax on as many citizens as possible. By 1970, Federal tax revenue was $192 billion. **In 2010, it was $2.1 trillion.**

DEDUCTION EXCEPTIONS AND FRAUD

Any two people making the same amount of money rarely pay the same amount of taxes. This is due to occupation, accountant, business expenses, dependents, state of health and thousands of other legal ways to reduce the tax burden. In the 95 years since the income tax was ratified, the tax law has grown into a separate, illogical, incomprehensible stack of rulings, decisions, and codes. The commissioner of the IRS readily admits he has never read all of the tax codes. The ordinary citizen is understandably bewildered by the contradictions in the law. Special interest groups constantly besiege the House Ways and Means Committee each time tax bills are being written. Depletion allowances for oil, reinvestment credits for industry, energy credits for the population and entertainment credits for businesses permit certain types of activities for certain people. But for the vast majority of the population, the entire matter is too complex.

The entire tax preparation industry, H.R. Block and the thousands of top notch accountants and lawyers became a necessary expense for even those people with modest incomes. The 1040 form with the appropriate supplementary forms for itemized deductions, capital gains and losses, supplemental income, social security self-employment tax and so on can only be filled out by a professional. And it has created an industry of tax preparation software that still throws ultimate responsibility back on the taxpayers to properly comply with all laws.

Today, one cannot pay a doctor's bill, receive a bonus, win a prize, buy or sell property, sign an alimony agreement, draw up a lease, establish a trust, exterminate termites or die without setting in train certain consequences of professional interest – to the IRS accountants and auditors.

If the income tax was used merely to collect taxes, the laws would be more equitable. But legislators and special interests, over the years, have tried to use it as a system of social change and discipline. Often the desired end cannot be accomplished through taxation but the resulting confusion in tax cases mires the noblest of reasons.

The law is so complex that the IRS does not stand behind the information it gives the taxpayer at its own offices. So by trying to comply by allowing the IRS to prepare the return, the taxpayer is still not assured of a correct return. The *Catch-22* is inescapable. The government mentality is, naturally, to gather as much money as is possible by the law. Fully aware of the large underground economy, its agents assume the taxpayer is guilty until he proves himself innocent. This means full documentation for every claimed deduction must be presented before a claim may be decided on. This reversal of role strikes terror into the most stout American hearts because we are not a nation of accurate bookkeepers. Innocent until proven guilty, the foundation of our legal system does not apply to tax audits. This assumption of guilt provides the government agents with an advantage no other law enforcement agency possesses, and it deprives the average American of any pretense that income taxes are paid voluntarily.

This assumption of guilt has made the IRS audit and subsequent (sometimes) trial for evasion one of the most dreaded public spectacles. The celebrity or whoever usually loses because of a flaw in interpretation of the law by the celebrity's' attorney or accountant. If the Commissioner of the IRS doesn't know the law, if the clerk in the IRS doesn't know the law, how can anyone know the law? The tax law is not a matter of whether you steal money; it is strictly a matter of how you do it, how well you play the system or if they can catch you. While the government takes money in the name of the social good, it contributes thick layers of fat to the body politic.

But the IRS is not a faceless giant; rather it is an organization of people, who for a variety of reasons make human errors. The first revenue agents were paid a commission on what they could collect from the public. That led to actual robbery and considerable theft. In 1953, the Commissioner of IRS was sent to jail as well as an assistant attorney general and the President's appointments secretary. Over the years, numerous mayors, judges, and elected officials have been sent to jail for evasion. But the Service itself has often abused the public. Routine payoffs, extortion, embezzlement and tax cases suppressed like traffic tickets were the ways of doing business in 1951.

The Nixon White House used the IRS to take care of its political opponents with the famous "enemies list." No matter what safeguards Congress chooses to install in the law, the nature of the information and the pressures of the job make the IRS a perfect vehicle for abuse. Most cases are decided in the privacy of the audit. Most taxpayers have more to conceal or think they have more to conceal from the tax man. Working at this disadvantage, the taxpayer is usually more than willing to make the deal, pay a little more in additional taxes and have the case closed.

Though revenue agents are no longer paid on the percentage of taxes they collect, collection is still the yardstick by which IRS officers are measured and promoted. So there is considerable pressure on the field officer to collect some money from every audit. Since the law is sufficiently complex that nearly any deduction can be challenged, the IRS agent always has power to disallow a deduction. That forces the taxpayer to pay the tax, and if he considers the deduction to be legitimate, he can sue for the return of the money. The time, expense and chances of winning are overwhelming stacked in favor of the government; in most cases it is not worth the trouble to fight the system. But individuals often choose the hard way, and that inherent rebellious streak and individualistic self-confidence of the American people is the fuel of the underground economy. Our self-pride is the strength of the nation and the bane of the taxman.

Though there is a tacit acceptance of paying tax on <u>some</u> money, the percentage is decreasing as government spending forces an inflation tax on the middle and lower classes of Americans. The Democratic Party policy that has constantly advocated higher taxes and higher tax rates on success is breaking apart in the harsh light of the tremendous cost of big government. Centralized authority, even if by the "best and the brightest" works against the grain of American productivity.

PROMISES PROMISES

No politicians can be elected on a platform of higher taxes. Yet in a bi-yearly ritual, the mating dance of the new Congress, taxes are juggled so that the government makes some concessions to one group while raising taxes on a much larger group. Often, with political cunning, politicians put off the effect of their votes for years, until AFTER the next election. Their hope is that the electorate will forget or they can deny they voted for it. The 1979 Congress increased the Social Security tax on nearly every working American but scheduled the increase to go into effect in January 1981, two months after the general election. Recent healthcare law started giving away benefits immediately but tax increases do not go into effect until after the 2012 presidential election.

Every election year promises of tax cuts have become the harbingers of winter betrayal. Government has become the most reckless and irresponsible consumer of the national wealth. In 1962, the government proposed the first $100,000,000,000 budget. From the ratification of the Constitution through the two largest wars ever fought by mankind, $100 billion dollars was the total operating budget for the all United States governments. Nine years later, after the Vietnam War the budget passed $200 billion in 1971.

Four years later it reached $300 billion, and only 2 years later in 1977 the budget was $400 billion.

Each election year, politicians promised better and cheaper government. Every president since Nixon has promised smaller government, but the 2011 national debt should reach over **$13.56** trillion dollars. The frightening aspect of the growth of the budget is the fatal disease of debt.

Ordinary taxpayers can see the rampant mismanagement and waste at the highest levels of government. The intelligent response to irresponsible government spending is resistance. Tax rebellion is a current and deeply seated feeling in Americans as the tax revolts at the state levels have proved. But the silent "majority" of Americans prefer the less obvious and more effective way to change personal taxation: by avoidance.

Political grandstanding and cries of un-American behavior echo from the lips of politicians these hollow promises of reform are greeted with cynical amusement by the public. The growth of the underground economy is a result of political actions in Washington. Profligate spending and an incomprehensible pile of exceptions and special cases have undercut the authority of Washington. The concept often repeated in the press that lower taxes will <u>cost</u> the government money is a bold-face lie. It is not the government's money; it is the individual taxpayer's money. Lower taxes will cost the taxpayer less for the privilege of paying for government.

By taking a page from our revolutionary past, American taxpayers are taking the problem of over-taxation into their own hands. Working out of sight of the collector is a direct and effective way to reduce personal taxes. Penalizing work and thrift makes no sense to the average man; and we are a sensible people.

III
VALUE ADDED

"In general, the art of government consists in taking as much money as possible from one party of the citizens to give to the other."

Voltaire

Skilled hands are used to produce reported and unreported income. In legal occupations, most of the transactions take place between individuals. By nature, such occupations as construction, repairs, crafts and services present opportunities for the ambitious individual. The limiting factors are time and will, not any profound social obstacles. In even the most primitive of societies, the person who develops the manual dexterity and will to fashion products with his hands is an asset to the community and to himself. Today, just as in medieval villages, the carpenters, masons, cobblers, bakers, candle makers contribute their skills and time to make products.

One of the basic economic laws of a product's value is directly related to the account of labor and time invested in transforming the item from non-useful to useful purposes. The rate at which this value is added, plotted against time, is the productivity rate of the worker. Though most productive work is now highly formalized in corporate structures, individual initiative and will continue to create items for use.

When sold in the free market, the individual and the society reap the benefits. Home industries from potting to macramé, music lessons to computer programming have gained rapid followings in the post-industrial return to cottage industries. The alternative lifestyles and cost of commuting are adding converts to do-it-yourself projects for cash. For many people, the added income is an extension of daily life, mainly weekend or evening work. These extra hours devoted to work, not leisure, are the essential ingredients of the success.

There are various degrees of sophistication and profitability involved with skilled work. There are some tradesmen who deliberately go on unemployment for part of the year while picking up jobs on the side. These underemployed are discussed in another chapter. No matter who you are, there are any number of skills, readily saleable, which can be acquired with some effort and training. Selling for cash, either before or after the project is complete is easier than most people think. And for the most part, the skills are in demand by people who want to save money yet obtain quality.

The contracting of work, freelance, is probably the largest source of under-reported income in the country. It is always cheaper, for both buyer and seller, because it cuts out the administrative overhead of government. Cash also eliminates finance, cash flow and collection costs.

Freelance work (derived from the medieval knight who rode from tournament to tournament selling his services to the highest bidder) is used extensively by small and medium size concerns that can't afford or have insufficient work to hire someone full time. The employer has no obligation to deduct withholdings or other taxes from the check but does report the income to the IRS on the 1099 form.

By using a contract, the basis of American business, both buyer and seller are protected. Contracts are enforceable in the courts (though with considerable delay) and provide details of the job expected and to be performed.

Verbal contracts, once the backbone of honorable business, still exist throughout the underground economy. Whether because of a fear of things on paper, a naivety of motivation, or just laziness, many transactions are done on the old-fashioned basis of word. Cash payments, of course, are a considerable inducement to trust.

CONSTRUCTION

A lucrative, concealable, and durable line of work is in the construction industry. Because of the nature of the business, with untitled heavy equipment worth hundreds of thousands of dollars, unexpected costs, cash transactions for subcontractors, labor racketeering, and multi-million dollar deals, big time evasion is rampant.

And with low-bidding the rule of the game, money is on and off the books and is as necessary to construction as grease. Building also buries most of the evidence so getting caught for including and not including items is impossible to detect. Specification revisions, errors, substitute materials and so forth make most large construction contracts read like cuneiform scrolls. The architect, let alone the IRS, has difficultly determining what actually went into the building.

The acceptance of this loose arrangement extends down to the ordinary laborer or skilled subcontractor like electrician, plumber, mason, plasterer, painter, carpenter, and roofer. Notoriously bad at keeping books, generally self-employed, always pressed for money, these contractors rather make a deal on certain aspects of construction. This is especially true in faster-growing areas of the country where the labor force is transient and the market follows boom-bust cycles.

Established firms keep records and comply with government regulations, but the necessity of having cash cannot be avoided if you intend on staying in business. A second set of books, tax books, is often necessary, especially for those just beginning in the business.

Johnny is a contractor who does interior framing and sheetrock work in Chicago. And he works as often as he can. Normally, Johnny has two types of jobs going, union jobs and off the books jobs.

On the union jobs where he must hire union men, the pay scale is from $20 to 40 an hour. Rules are strictly enforced on the job site and there are no ends to the jurisdictional disputes among unions which sometimes close down the job for hours or days. But these jobs are financed by major banks and are bankrolled for $3 million or more. Johnny often gets the contracts by doing "favors" for general contractors or specific sub-contractors who will include Johnny in the job bid.

But this doesn't always work, because there is a lot of competition for these high priced jobs. So Johnny has an arrangement with several developers who renovate apartment buildings. He began working as a sub for them in the bust construction market in the early 90s. Now, they use him whenever they can and he often lines up other tradesmen for the developer.

Why? On these jobs, Johnny pays and is paid in cash. At the end of the week, he is paid for the work done. And he never has any trouble finding workmen. Several of the men on his regular union crew work off the books for Johnny while collecting unemployment because there are no union jobs available. So in addition to the $225 in unemployment benefits, these guys make $300-400/week working for Johnny without paying any withholding, social security or income taxes. They are fast, experienced and employed. Though they are making $5-8 an hour less than a union job, they bring home about the same money. But Johnny also hires a number of illegals, mostly Hispanic, sometimes Polish or Irish, for minimum wage or just above. He feels he's helping them earn a living in the city while saving him and the developer money. The illegals are happy to have the work and grateful for the cash pay envelope each week. And the developer, who has been in the business for years, keeps a source of cash because he can reduce the construction expense of the project by 15-20 percent by paying cheaper subs in cash and avoiding costly labor disputes. When he sells the units as condominiums, he will not report one or two of the units which will supply him with cash for the next job. And the cycle continues.

At the commercial level, this type of relationship is wrought with hazards of breach of contract, payment disputes and alike. In order to get around this but still maintain the "cash" mentality of the work, a developer will permit the contractor to inflate the amount and/or cost of labor being put into the building. The developer takes those artificially high costs and deducts them from his sale price thus reducing his taxable income. The contractor, who doesn't declare any (or part) of the project gets a cash kickback from the developer. Once again, the government middleman is cut out of the deal. And once the building is finished, who knows if 500 or 800 2x4 studs were used in the walls?

Construction schemes are more prevalent in the boom markets where competition for skilled labor and fast completion encourages shady deals.

On the individual level, construction holds the best prospects for large, unearned income. Every homeowner, at one time or another, has needed repairs to the house, has made additions, or upgraded the look. Since most of these contracts are one time affairs, the legitimate guy who will do the job during normal business hours must charge for his overhead, taxes, and other business costs.

But there is always someone around who is ambitious enough to do the work on the weekend or in the evening. This is especially true for such non-essentials as finishing a basement, remodelling a bath, insulating the attic, painting the exterior or paneling the playroom.

Ernie, a middle-aged home improvement contractor in Ohio, has been working on and off the books most of his life. He is married with three children and lives in a modest suburban home. But he didn't begin that way.

After high school, he joined the army where he learned to read blueprints. When he was discharged he began working as a carpenter's assistant. Ambitious, he often would work for his boss on Saturday as well. When winter came, he went on unemployment but was quickly bored by not working. Hearing about jobs in Florida, he and a friend moved south and quickly found work. They stayed there for the winter, being paid in cash while collecting unemployment in Ohio. In late spring, they returned home and went back to work. In five years, Ernie had saved enough from his off the books job that he went into business for himself.

Still a compulsive worker, but a poor bookkeeper, Ernie continues working off the books doing kitchen remodeling, basement finishing and other items for homeowners. His reputation is pretty good, and his prices for this weekend work allow some of his neighbors who didn't think they could afford it, to have the work done. He is a regular church goer and belongs to the local American Legion post. Many of the jobs are referrals from other customers or from community contacts by his family and friends. Ernie is not abusive about the income he doesn't declare. From his primary business, he has an accountant and he pays his local and state taxes on time. But he is convinced that if he had not begun hustling jobs on the side, he could never have afforded the house, car or tuition for college. His wife is totally ignorant of taxes and he doesn't feel comfortable with the forms either. He doesn't trust any politician with money especially for those expensive social programs. Any qualms he had about the off the books jobs have been dispelled by the constant inflation. After twenty five years of working, he feels that he is losing ground and wonders if he can ever afford to retire.

Inherent in the reasoning by most people who construct permanent buildings with their hands is the realization that the value of their work will far outlive then. They recognize that their contribution to the economic fabric will increase in value with time, as can be seen in homes they have provided for most Americans.

IRS officials, of course, know that many contractors of all ilks are notorious for their concealable income. And they are regularly scrutinized for disparities between their receipts and their declared income. But when the deal is made for cash, the contractor may give a receipt to the customer, but rarely does he keep that receipt for himself. It's just evidence against him.

There have always been the contractors, urban, suburban, rural and semi-rural areas who pay no taxes on any work they do. Handymen, fly-by-night contractors, journeymen, odd-jobbers have been part of the American economy since the founding of the country. That many of them can't, won't or don't keep books doesn't mean they are getting rich off the system. Mostly, they are just getting by, comfortably in some cases, but certainly not getting rich.

The largest area of growth in the construction business is coming from women who, with the proliferation of carpentry, plumbing, wiring and other home construction courses are finding ways to augment income by doing those simple jobs for neighbors and friends. With divorce common, single mothers find that the flexible arrangement such jobs give them, permit mothering as well as working. Though not wide-spread yet, growing familiarity with do-it-yourself projects has spurred the growth of interest in women at places like Home Depot.

REPAIRS

The first cousin to building is repairing. Until the rapid expansion of the economy after World War II, repairing useful items rather than throwing them away was as ingrained in our fabric as the Franklin adage of "a stitch in time saves nine." But advertising and the seemingly limitless expansion of our productive capacity made the throw away culture synonymous with the American way of life.

Depending on the amount of time and type of repair work, the chances of being detected are slim. The auto mechanic who works on Saturday or Sunday is well concealed unless he doesn't do quality work.

Quality becomes the important facet of repair work. Though every repair business depends on word of mouth advertising, negative comments can ruin the underground business if some foul tempered individual decides to report it to the IRS. While paranoia is a major contribution of the tax man to the American frame of mind, his threat is louder than his bite.

Ira is retired now in Sun City, Arizona after 35 years of work, mostly for General Electric in Syracuse. He was the son of immigrant parents. His father died when Ira was 14 and he ran errands and made deliveries for small manufacturers. His fascination with electric motors began when he rode on the electric trolley and saw a moving picture. Then he began working for the granddaddy of electric companies. And on the side, in those few spare hours he had to himself, he tinkered with broken machines. And he was good at fixing them. Word spread to the neighborhood, and soon, Ira was fixing little items in exchange for barter goods like clothes, food and good will.

After the Second World War, the neighborhood changed and Ira moved with his family to a suburban home, small tract houses which mushroomed around the major cities after the war. He still worked hard at his job but the demand for repair work exploded with the host of household items which appeared on the market. Now Ira was taking cash for his work because barter was no longer needed. The extra money he earned was directed to his children's education, an evening out with his wife, a new barbeque and assorted items of the good life over the years.

Now bald, 75 years old, he's itchy from a lifetime of work. His wife had wanted him to sell his "shop" before they moved west, but he couldn't part with those happy memories. Though she hasn't told him yet, the $500 a week he makes fixing motors, pumps and other assorted electric items has kept them close to inflation rather than falling into poverty as they grow older.

The case is being repeated in St. Petersburg, San Diego, Fort Meyers and Charleston as well as in other clusters of older Americans around the country. Some cases are being perpetuated, passed from generation to generation as every learned skill should be. But the generation of immigrants almost took for granted that a person had to work two jobs, seven days a week to earn enough money to stay alive. Taxes were taken out at work or on services like post office, cigarettes, liquor, and imports. It wasn't that long ago men were respected for their desire to work. Concealing income wasn't the motivation, success was. And, it's better than working as a bagger in the local grocery store.

Tony was the oldest boy in a family of 12 children from north of Naples, Italy. At age 14, in 1916 he left Naples alone on a ship in the last wave of southern European immigration. He got a job carrying water to Italian laborers on a bridge project in New Jersey and gathered pieces of coal which fell from the freight cars at night. There were still horse trolleys in the street.

His ambition and the opportunity of America kept Tony going each day, 18 to 20 hours. As he moved up on the construction crew, he constantly learned and at night, for a dollar a week, he would tend boilers in the sub-basements, shovelling coal and having a free place to stay. He didn't mind because that extra dollar was important. The term "off the books" was yet to be coined and the 16th Amendment wasn't aimed at his level of minimum wages. Social security, even unions, were still years away. But through sweat and continuous work, this nearly illiterate immigrant boy raised a family sending all three of his children through college. He didn't borrow money, paid his debts and spent half his life in the underground economy.

Tony cannot understand that the repair work he did on heavy machinery, for cash on completion, was illegal. He was the proudest of Americans, proud of his ability to read the language, of the opportunity the country gave him to prosper. His sons went to war, and he voted in every election, He cannot understand when the government tells you that you are a criminal for working, for doing, for building.

He worked on the great construction projects of New Jersey, the refineries, bridges, tunnels, highways. He worked and worked always believing he was contributing. And he paid his taxes. His ignorance of the scope of the tax laws and the interpretations by the IRS never caught up with Tony. But for the more educated generation, a constant fear of being "caught" for working or being penalized for that ambition for a better life have helped to dull the edge of desire.

There is that core of American ambition, the land of economic opportunity, which in reality drew far more immigrants than the abstract notions of democracy or religious freedom. The right to succeed or fail, large or small, is fundamental to the true purpose of our democracy. By restricting the titled inheritance of power, by granting wide avenues to success, the United States is unique in the history of man. The bureaucratization of the economic life, begun at the turn of the 20th Century has reached the level of maturation. The numbing forms of compliance are trying to make bookkeepers out of workers. Tony and Ernie lived their lives when the world was less complicated, before the airplane, television and the high speed computer which checks statistical deviations from the norm.

Work was achievement and it is that basic ingredient which persists in both construction and repair work. The reward is paid after the effort achieves. For the most part, the risk is personal without the help or support of the government. The rewards are limited by the person's ability, inclination and talent at working.

ARTS AND CRAFTS

The explosion in American crafts, rediscovered in the recent years provides an outlet for thousands of creative Americans while boosting the income. With the basic survival needs met, in most cases, through legitimate work, these hobbies are working their way into the fabric of the home in much the same way they did during the 18th and 19th centuries. Traditional female crafts have undergone the most profound changes as the social mobility of women has taken them out of the home and into the office and factory. Quilting, crocheting, knitting, needlepoint, macramé, canning, pottery, candle making, weaving, caning, and less glamorous items have developed into a therapy from the grind of daily work as well as a source of artistic and monetary reward.

As part of the search for some economic independence, especially in the less metropolitan areas (or exurbia as some demographers call it), time is not mindlessly wasted in the deadening light of the TV screen. Trends which found resurgence in California and Colorado during the late 90's are taking on an economic significance for many families. Since family sizes as a rule have decreased, the stay at home mother, more cognizant of her creative ability has put her talents to use.

In suburban Atlanta, Cheryl is a 28 year old mother of two young children. College educated at the University of Georgia, she worked as a secretary until she married her husband, a freight traffic manager. While still in college, Cheryl learned to macramé plant holders, wall hangings, vests and assorted objects.

Without putting any time constraints on her, Cheryl weaves between 100 and 150 items a year, in between her chores of housekeeping and child rearing. As she finishes each item, she puts it away in her closet until the first of December when she rents a booth at an indoor flea market near Atlanta. By Christmas, she has over $3,000 for her casual crafts and hundreds of people have inexpensive, one of a kind presents under their Christmas trees.

Cheryl didn't begin weaving as an occupation. It was more of an escape and diversion while she was pregnant with her first child. But her energy soon filled the house and she began running out of friends and relatives to give items to. That's when her girlfriend suggested that she try to sell them. It took her two years to go from the suggestion to the flea market but now she looks forward to the yearly marketing of her handicraft. Is she worried that the IRS will catch her for her income? No. In fact, Cheryl is oblivious to the rules she is breaking. To her, it is a hobby not an occupation. And besides, she never felt comfortable with numbers.

In reality, if Cheryl decided to approach her crafts enterprise as a business, it would probably be awash after she took into account the cost of her materials, transportation (which she does during her errands), storage, inventory, booth rental, telephone, home workshop, capital borrowing (from her husband), and accounting help not to mention salary for herself. If her business acumen was that sharp, she would have a string of cottage industries, fleets of trucks and thousands of booths set up nationwide to market her handicrafts. But that isn't her intent. And though she may show a net profit if she took all her legal deductions, a truly aggressive accountant might devise a business loss which could then be deducted from her husband's tax return.

If the IRS for some reason audited the family return ($80,000 yearly, filled out by H.R. Block with standard deductions for mortgage, medical and two dependents) and found out about Cheryl's hobby, they would assess the tax and penalty without figuring her business expenses because she has no receipts. That experience would end Cheryl's yearly trips to the market, perhaps her craft entirely. She might return to giving her work away or to the local church bazaar where she could deduct the entire amount from her husband's return as charitable contribution. The end result would be either a decrease in taxable income or a reduction of productive capacity. The Catch-22 nature of the situation does not affect the IRS perception; the enforcement of the rules as they are written is the only guiding factor, no matter how illogical.

Tiny enterprises like Cheryl's abound throughout the country. With gross incomes under $7,000, the actual net worth of most of these projects, using the sophisticated accounting techniques employed by large conglomerates would show a tax loss for the first five years and only a minimal profit thereafter. Small time craftsmen are usually less certain that their products will sell than they are of proper business procedures. The Small Business Administration estimates that 50 percent of new businesses fail in the first year. And these are the properly set up businesses, the ones which plan to observe all of the rules, regulations, filing deadlines, withholdings and other paperwork incumbent on any business person.

Strict IRS interpretation of the law classifies these evaders the same as the larger, more sophisticated projects like Johnny the New York City contractor. Though the result may be the same, evasion of tax on part of the income, the scale and the overlooked legitimate deductions makes enforcement at this level not cost effective for the government.

SERVICE

In the post-industrial America, service occupations such as computer programming, software development, website designer, illustration, graphics, architectural design, photography and music are among the host of desired skills which are readily employed on a freelance basis. Upper crust consultants in management, energy, marketing, time management and alike have also blossomed under a fee paid, fixed time contracts.

These white collar, self-employed professionals under-report income or file no returns at all. Most are paid by ordinary business check and a 1099 form is sent to the government. Or the employer lists the service as a simple purchase, throwing the responsibility and paperwork back to the individual. In either case, it is up to the individual to tally up his/her income and pay quarterly self-employment tax, social security tax, withholding and sales tax. But the IRS receives over 63 million pieces of information on paper each year. Physically it is impossible for them to match incoming information with tax returns. The weight of numbers is on the side of the contractor.

The simple business purchase of services is the cleanest way for both business and individual to circumvent all of the paperwork of employment. By treating the contract the same way as a purchase order for a desk, lumber, office supplies, etc. the purchaser carries the cost of the John Doe Consulting Firm under purchases not under employment. The cost of the service is fully tax deductible for the purchaser as a business expense, so he doesn't care what the individual does with his tax return. The purchaser is not in the enforcement business for the IRS.

Of course, this bookkeeping practice has large legitimate applications in the business community. Consulting firms employing hundreds of people are run in the normal business fashion. It is the one or two man shops, who because of marginal profitability or lack of manpower, do not comply with the letter of the law. And their employers, also small shops who can't afford to hire help full time, are happy to be relieved of the added expense of withholdings and government reporting.

Mark is a 30 year old web designer in Dallas who recently emigrated from Chicago where he had worked for a number of publishing companies. His 29 year old girl friend Elaine is a copy editor/proof reader. When they first arrived in Texas, they both thought it would be easy to find jobs in their respective fields since each of them had good corporate experience. But industry in Texas was neither as concentrated nor as well paying as it was in Chicago. Mark began taking freelance assignments from advertising agencies that did corporate reports, brochures, publicity pieces and assorted print materials. He was paid as a freelancer with 1099 forms. Within a short period of time, he became friendly with an artist who had many small customers, new businesses and low volume businesses which also needed websites but couldn't afford the cost of an agency. Mark began picking up these jobs directly and getting paid as a separate company. Elaine, in the meantime, was finding spin-off work from Mark, writing copy but more frequently rewriting the sloppy prose of the restaurateurs, plumbing wholesalers and small retailers.

Neither of them had ever intended on going into business as such, and with their lack of business experience, they neither incorporated nor kept very accurate records of expenses or income. Most of the money which came in was immediately spent and they both thought it easier not to file any return than try and figure out their complicated financial situation. Since they had moved from Illinois to

Texas, they felt comfortable that the tax man would not be able to trace them. And they both cringed at the thought of the major expense in April of a check to the government. Taking the juvenile approach rather than consulting an accountant who might shelter their income, Mark and Elaine simply dropped into the underground economy.

THE WORK ETHIC

Taking money from skill developed by years of practice and patience seems to be in the best interest of the country. Paying taxes on that earned income sounds reasonable because individuals who work should pay taxes to support the government. The counterbalance to this reasoning is the complexity and cost of complying with paying taxes. In those marginally profitable lines of repairs, arts and crafts and some services, not paying taxes is the only way these activities manage to survive. The IRS contention that everyone who engages in a skill should be an accountant as well flies in the face of reality. America was built on sweat equity coming from those people who worked 16 to 20 hours a day to build a dream. It is that quality of character that keeps the ambitious and talented people working "in" America rather than fleeing to more inviting shores. And it is that opportunity to work which has drawn the boldest of the world's population to our shores.

The celebrated brain drain to the United States from around the world was acknowledgement of the fundamental right Americans have to work and prosper. While the little guy works with his hands and mind to produce prosperity for his family, he lives with certain guilt, knowing that he doesn't know how to pay taxes on that money. He knows it is "wrong" but the distrust of government and politicians has grown so rapidly that the individual has only one protest, working for himself in his spare time.

The productive use of time, no matter how many taxes are not directly paid on the products, contributes to the economic advancement of the country. While evading unfathomable income tax codes can be soundly decried from every pulpit, it overlooks the real decline in American productivity which would accompany the enforcement of the rules. Skilled hands produce out of a type of love;

a love of achievement, a sense of pride, a feeling of completion, a desire for betterment. The intrusion of the government hand into this process is understandable but can be destructive. Balancing the social responsibility of the government and the moral responsibility of the individual to the government is the crux of the problem. And that line, like the shifting beach, is constantly changing.

IV

HORSE TRADING

"The hardest thing in the world to understand is the income tax."

Albert Einstein

Since the beginning of organized societies governments have cast covetous eyes on the wealthy merchant and trader classes. Middlemen always seem to have wealth which eludes kings and tyrants. As easily identifiable sources of wealth, traders from the Phoenicians to the Jewish merchants were persecuted for their success at bringing the imponderable differences of culture and societies together at a profit for themselves. Taxation inevitably follows success.

The American consumer is no longer buying sustenance but luxury. Poverty as the ancients knew it does not exist in our country. We have made progress in food, medicine communications and perceptions that affect the most isolated of our countrymen.

The role of trader and merchant throughout history was instrumental in the material advantages we enjoy today. But as a readily indefinable source of wealth every ruler imposed taxes on the trading class. The American Revolution was begun by the unhappy merchant classes in Boston, Philadelphia and Virginia over the basic question of taxation and another revolution is taking shape around the same question.

As often as the tax gatherer attempted to gain the upper hand over the merchant, the merchants of the world found ways around him. Though our institutional compliance factor has reduced the taxman's job, the small shopkeeper is recognized by the IRS as a problem taxpayer. Yet small business is the backbone of the American economy. While most taxpaying in the merchant field is institutionalized, the constant demand of government for more information, as well as the unnecessary intrusion of OSHA, FTC, DOE, and EPA, has saddled the little guy with endless "compliance" paperwork.

The merchants of the country are as elusive as 19th Century peddlers. Making a buck requires hard work, much of it travel time or capital invested in hard goods that must be sold. When the Crown put the stamp taxes on imported goods, patriotic Americans like John Hancock and other merchants quite reasonably resorted to smuggling goods in order to avoid the taxes.

Literally billions of commercial transactions occur each year in this country making most impossible for the government to monitor. Fixed commercial establishments like Macy's or Walmart handle the large volume and manage the paperwork for the government. But in the last twenty years, the old fashioned bazaar, now called a flea market, re-established itself in most communities around the country. The first cousin to this people's market is the familiar "garage sale". And with the online market place of E-bay and Craigslist has expanded the marketplace to the world. Now in any part of the country, in fact the world, if you have something to sell, there is a marketplace to sell it. Those people, who buy, collect, distribute or otherwise understand the value of products, can make a living from their chair.

Each Saturday and Sunday, millions of people flock to Paducah, Kentucky or the sprawling market in Denver, Colorado looking for bargains or to gain extra cash. No item is too old, exotic, or commonplace not to have a potential buyer. Loading up the van or car, paying the five or ten dollar exhibitor's fee, and spending the day meeting folks is a reversion to simpler times, before malls, credit cards and blister packed wrapped goods. The self-expression is worth hundreds of millions of dollars when multiplied by the countless cities and towns.

Evelyn is a retired homemaker, as she calls herself, who lives in Aurora, Colorado, a suburb of Denver. Her husband died two years ago and both of her children are married. Three days a week she works as a practical nurse at a local hospital. The rest of the week she shops garage sales, thrift shops and auctions. On Saturday and Sunday, she and Tuffy, her 10 year old terrier, are at their regular spot at the flea market. Evelyn makes between $15,000 and 20,000 a year buying and selling, but she put many years into refining her techniques.

Originally, she began going to garage sales to buy household goods for her family, especially in the hard times after her second child was born. Later, it became a more than a necessity, and it was her social integration back into society after her husband's death. She sold the house to move into an apartment so she didn't have to do the heavy maintenance. A sinewy farm girl from Nebraska, she married at 17, out of high school. The years of earlier poverty aged her face with a wisdom and will. During the sale, the real estate broker took care of all of the details, but Evelyn wanted to sell the household items and buy new furniture for the new apartment. One Saturday, summoning her courage, she and her son loaded a rented truck. For 10 hours on Saturday and Sunday she watched her old life turn into cash. More, than that, she enjoyed the interaction with people. Evelyn made over $2,000 that first day which got her hooked on the life.

When Evelyn goes to a garage sale, she watches out for the professionals who run weekly sales, just as she runs her weekly booth at the flea market. The genuine people want to get rid of the 'junk' they are selling. One strategy she uses is to slowly walk around the yard, putting all the items she wants into one pile. Then she offers, a price for everything, say 20 dollars. This strategy works very well in the late afternoon, when the people are tired and more than happy to convert goods into money rather than having to lug them back inside.

She tries to get people talking about why things are on sale: moving, death, housecleaning, wanting some extra cash, etc. This gives her an edge in her negotiations. And she learned to use the well timed walk away to bring the price down.

Earl is also a flea market devotee. But Earl only handles new goods which he buys at wholesale or below. He tries to stay with household goods like pillows, sheets, towels and clothing. A former salesman for a national dry goods firm, he tried his own business, selling the same close-out items from a fixed location. But the overhead and bookkeeping were killing him while he discovered that most customers were reluctant to buy close-out items, feeling there was something wrong with them.

After six months, the store failed and Earl carted the rest of his merchandise to the flea market where he discovered his market. In a few hours his "new" goods were snatched up and he did no bookkeeping when he got home.

Four years later, his new business is still going strong. Earl watches the newspaper classified for close-out items, speaks to several manufacturers reps on a regular basis, and stays in touch with most of the major wholesale houses in his area. Operating the same way he did when he ran the store, Earl tries to guess what his customers are in the market for. Sweaters and rugs in the fall are stocked, beach towels and shorts in the spring. His garage is his warehouse and his camper is his store. This time, his business is successful and he spends no time working for the government.

Next to Earl each week is Aaron, the Mennonite farmer, who sells 35 varieties of homemade cheese. And across the way are Sally and Steve, young jewelry makers, who always sell an assortment of original and old jewelry. In fact, of the 150 places rented each weekend, over 125 of them go to regular customers, None of them pay sales tax, income tax, social security self-employment tax, unemployment compensation, corporation tax or any other kind of tax. It is strictly a cash business, done in the ancient, moveable market. Though the government might want to collect taxes on these transactions, enforcement would be too costly and time consuming. Practically, there could never he enough taxmen to cover all of the flea markets in the country.

With the advent of the internet, the "flea market" went viral. All sorts of hobbyists from baseball cards to beer can collectors can get together to buy and sell goods. Specialty hobby groups who know the value of products to the individual allow increases in value as well as satisfying people's desire for certain goods. One beer can collection was sold for $25,000 after having been amassed over 20 years of collecting in flea markets and trading with others. The IRS never got its share.

Craigslist has become a replacement for the classified ads and allows people to dispose of all sorts of household items from large screen televisions to kayaks. Neatly arranged by geographic location, buyers and sellers can decide how far and how much people are will to pay for certain items. It also works as a marketplace to price items to a real time market. Almost no one declares their income from Craigslist.

COMMISSIONED SALES

While the travelling salesman is the butt of many jokes, the amount of unreported income is no laughing matter to the revenue service. Commission checks routinely paid to salesmen on a quarterly basis often do not have taxes withheld. The burden of reporting is left to the individual who in many cases is less than accurate in his reporting.

Independence of action is the key to this arrangement; it permits the salesman to work for himself. Though many firms employ salesmen directly, many more hire them as independents. The manufacturer's rep is the cleverest of this group, having many masters but beholding to none. He uses as business expenses most of his travel and entertainment while paying minimal money in taxes.

Jim, age 35, is a manufacturer's rep who works out of Ogden, Utah. His territory extends from Montana to Arizona so he spends a good deal of time on the road. While Jim began in business at a normal salary plus commission jobs, he soon became wise to the broad areas of growth. As rep for a number of different manufacturers, Jim receives his checks as an independent contractor thereby avoiding withholding taxes. Knowing full well that he must declare some of his income, Jim shows the normal business expenses and he declares a fair living to the government. But the numerous small accounts are the gravy for his operation. Paid by check, Jim simply cashes the checks to avoid leaving a record against his bank account.

But being a building supply salesman over that large of an area, especially in the West, provides Jim with numerous opportunities to buy and sell other things. Knowing many of the wholesalers throughout the area, Jim acts to help balance the market by getting the material to the place it can be sold. If a dealer has a surplus of lumber in Albuquerque and another guy in Colorado Springs needs some, Jim puts the deal together and gets three to eight percent commission in cash as a broker's fee. Naturally the money stays unreported.

In San Francisco, Sammy is a broker in the more traditional sense of the word. A third generation Chinese American, his family has engaged in the import-export business for fifty years. Dealing mainly in small items from China and Taiwan, the business shows a ledger as an importer with few if any exports. Sammy, however, sets up grain and scrap metal deals with the Orient for American exporters. Married with three grown children, one who just learned the business, Sammy received his MBA from Stanford. This side line, which occupies little of his time, is carried out through old school connections from college.

In the last two years, Sammy began moving into the field of cash transfers rather than product transfers because through electronic means, they can be carried out more efficiently and with less risk. Primarily, Sammy sets up loans from private foreign concerns in Singapore, Hong Kong and other Asian nations, in dollars, for the financing of shipments to and from the United States. Often he finds a guarantor of exports in Asia for an American concern which wants to import. Since all of the financing is done outside the scrutiny of American business regulations, higher interest rates, and stiffer terms can be applied to the riskier ventures. But the success pays off for Sammy whose "finder's fee" deposited in a Singapore bank is well out of the range of IRS auditors. The trading connections he works with were established by his grandfather who began importing wooden and cheap plastic toys from Hong Kong.

Through family connections, the international grandsons of the older traders have become sophisticated in ways to avoid the tax man. Liberal laws of business privacy in Hong Kong and Singapore aid the avoidance. Sammy is only one of the numerous traders from the Orient, Europe, South America and the Middle East who regularly supply the American market with goods. The huge amount of Euros and dollars deposited in foreign banks as well the currency-transfers of the huge multi-national corporation's further obscures the dealings of the smaller entrepreneurs.

BARTER

The first barter-transactions between people predate the Internal Revenue Service by more than 4000 years. The oldest form of exchange, the gain of goods and services is more in the mind of the trader than it is in the control of the market. When the Indians sold Manhattan Island to the Dutch for $24 of glass and metal beads, both sides thought they were receiving the fair market value. Today the IRS would have assessed both buyer and seller the full market value of the transaction even though no cash was exchanged and both parties agreed that the beads and other items were the correct value.

Barter exchange, however, is more difficult to detect than cash exchanges. Trying to quantify the goods would take an entire Federal bureau because millions of items are exchanged daily by people who do not want, do not need or have too much of one thing and not enough of another. In most countries, such exchanges are the private business of the individual, But the government in its fear of being cheated, insist that all barter arrangements be recorded for their market cash value.

A man is driving down the road and stops for a hitchhiker with a suitcase. They travel for five miles and the car breaks down. The hitchhiker, who is a mechanic, wants to get to the next town for a new job. In his suitcase he carried his tools. He fixes the fuel pump, and tunes up the engine and tightens the breaks. The driver drops the man at the next town which is 1.5 miles away.

The driver, according to the IRS, receives $50 of compensation income, for only about $4.00 of expense. The net gain to the driver is $46 which should be reported on his tax form.

The hitchhiker cannot declare the loss of his services to the tune of that $46. In a barter exchange, the individual is put on the line to make a decision. If he is wrong and gets the short end of the stick, he loses and the government refuses to recognize the loss. But if he wins, if he happens to make the right decision, drive a hard bargain, he is penalized by taxes. He is "obliged" to declare his success like some bar room braggart.

Naturally, no government could police these informal transactions but the Internal Revenue Service has been particularly interested in the organized barter clubs that have sprung up across the country since the mid-seventies. Organized barter clubs have grown to over 200 individual outlets across the country grossing over $150 million with an annual increase of 20percent a year forecast.

Demand for the services of these clubs comes mainly from small businesses which use the club to clear out unwanted inventory while obtaining credits for everything from office equipment to building materials. The clubs that try to maintain a high degree of secrecy (for obvious reasons) market member's products through newsletters and the internet. The national networks are under pressure to keep accurate records but the nature of the business, allows some broad estimates on what any product is worth at a given time.

Services, especially of professionals like doctors, lawyers, mechanics and skilled trades are always in demand in the barter economy. Exchanges are difficult and time consuming which makes barter work better in smaller towns and rural areas. Chickens for a legal fee were once the norm rather than the exception. Money was invented to facilitate market transactions, thus the reversion to the primitive transaction base should not worry our tax collectors. Barter is inexact relying more on specific personal needs than on the greater market value of the services or goods.

The barter system which begins when kids swap baseball cards or video games will never be adequately counted. Efforts to eliminate these transactions under the illusion of a "fairness" doctrine are impossible. Unless there is a revenuer in every kitchen, we will continue to trade with our neighbors and friends and like-minded individuals.

V

Fibbers and Finaglers

"The income tax has made more liars out of the American people than golf has."

Will Rogers

The massive avoidance of income tax is best seen in the exaggerated deductions many people take on their income taxes. This large "Who me?" conference activity is as old as the system which introduced the word "deduction" to daily usage. The temptation to cheat is unavoidable and complete honesty is economic lunacy. Even the best intentioned taxpayers find that documenting all of their legitimate deductions is often difficult because of simple carelessness.

Reducing the gross income to a smaller net income is the game every player strives to achieve. Thousands of accountants and lawyers are only too willing to help the taxpayer estimate how much he spent in every category of legal deductions. The IRS accentuates the game by using the Taxpayers Compliance Measurement Program (TCMP) to evaluate which returns deviate form a mean economic model for returns in a certain category. The IRS decides which is "normal" for every important item on a return according to income bracket and geographical demographics.

By establishing a model return, the IRS has set up guidelines for potential cheaters to use as a guidepost, especially those represented by decent accountants. Tax preparers will recommend that the taxpayer take certain deductions for charity, professional journals, union dues, energy credits and so forth which are in line with the taxpayers income bracket.

This is done with the knowledge that the IRS cannot audit every return, and in fact, will not audit returns with certain types and amount of deductions. This theory allows preparers to get the best deal for clients at income tax time.

The TCMP serves another important purpose, especially for the IRS by insuring its statistical base of "compliance" remains above 90percent of returns. This protects the service from political pressure and reform movements because the evidence of compliance by the voluntary tax payer looks excellent by the model's guide.

Introducing sophisticated programming and electronic filing to the tax process has made the IRS into a super agency able to leap tall mountains of data with a single button. Even with their old computers, the TCMP program is a significant weapon of the government.

With it, the government can select certain variables like profession, income level and geographic area. With a simple program, the auditor can pull all returns of dentists in Ohio earning $250,000 who took energy tax credits. Any combination of personal data can be used to pull any segment of the population.

The TCMP system has a built in cheating factor that determines how much a taxpayer can "get away with" before the amount is too much. $10,000 is the breakeven point where collection costs equal the amount of potential taxes due.

The program knows what the normal level of cheating is, and accepts that as the "normal" behavior of the population with statistical sampling. If you cheat less than the norm, the program awards you no points. But if you try to cheat above the norm, the program may kick you out so that an agent can examine your return. This becomes a game of statistical chance or 1 in 2000 likelihood of being audited. The numbers game and the total antiseptic quality of the process has propelled the government into a relationship of machines vs. humans with the human element already blind, deaf and dumb.

With these staggering odds facing the ordinary person, it would seem that the individual would shy away from conflict with the might of the government computers. But the urge for survival and prosperity is still sufficiently strong to fuel many attempts at getting away with it. As economic hard times increase, the cheating ratio for the population increases, making the "normal" dollar amount greater which puts the completely honest man further behind. Not fair, you say? In tax discussion, no one uses the word "fair." Taxes and fairness have little if any relationship and are, for the most part, mutually exclusive terms.

ENLARGING DEDUCTIONS

Everything costs more each year. Despite the economic news out of the Federal Reserve the cost of running a family increases each year. So it is only natural that we should enlarge the cost of legitimate deductions. Or fabricate deductions for a tax year.

-- *The Doctor Game* – Nearly everyone knows that medical expenses are tax deductible. Sickness and repeated trips to the doctor can save the taxpayer money. Naturally, this is a good thing. The government should want the taxpayer to get well and be able to contribute productive labor.

Healthy people are discriminated against so many invent doctors with the stroke of a keyboard. The law requires receipts for any doctor bills. Since most people know this requirement, they have evidence in the form of bills or canceled checks. The IRS knows this as well and it infrequently requires taxpayers to substantiate large medical claims. With relative security, a taxpayer or his accountant can claim a certain amount of medical deductions every year, regardless of the individual's state of heath.

For the more paranoid (or careful) taxpayer, it pays to be certain a receipt exists. This can be done so easily that it is nearly undetectable. Among your doctor bills is a $1525 check to Wilfred Martins, MD. When audited, the taxpayer provides the agent with a copy of the canceled check as proof of the deduction. The agent will look at the documentation and move on. In reality, however, Wilfred Martins is a local handyman who did work in the basement. After the canceled check was returned to the taxpayer, he simply added the letter "MD" after the name and filed the check away.

Playing this game requires nerve but the odds are in the favor of the taxpayer who has prepared well. The doctor scheme is limited in scope because of the percentage of gross income that needs to be impacted in order to claim any deduction. The frequent abuse by people familiar with it can lead to audits.

-- *The Larger Family* – Like the doctor bill, additional exemptions appear every year around tax time. If the census bureau used tax data to collect population figures, they would find millions of uncounted minors living around the country. It is simple to see why a person, pushed to the wall by economic hard times, when confronted with the tax form on April 14th, checks the box for dependents and adds his 28 year old son who lives in California or writes in Ralph, his spaniel as 12 years old.

Since the tax form requires Social Security numbers for all exemptions, this scheme has become a bit more difficult. But the number of fake Social Security numbers is enormous, or the use of a real one with a child who has left the house is virtually undetectable. However, if exemptions jump from 1 to 6 in a year, the taxpayer will set off alarms and needs to be ready to document the new "Brady Bunch" to the auditor.

-- *Theft and Casualty Loss* – The government doesn't expect a taxpayer to idly suffer the loss of goods because of criminal theft, fire, storms or acts of God. This leaves a large area for individuals to claim losses for any number of household goods like expensive jewelry.

Businesses, especially small ones, may resort to crime and casualty loss to bail them out of tough economic times. In addition to any insurance fraud, arson of premises or vehicles, disappearance of inventory or other merchandise allows straight line deductions on the corporate tax form. These claims increase during a recession because of the pressure of the business cycle. But inept or careless business people use it as an escape hatch from their mistakes.

A limiting factor to all types of casualty claims is that the government becomes very suspicious, as it should, if the claims happen with any regularity. Fraud of this type, when challenged by the government will result in the entire claim being disallowed – police report or not. In may be difficult for the IRS to prove a crime has been committed by the taxpayer. But punishing the taxpayer with the full tax liability is sufficient penalty for the tax man. Then the burden of proof shifts to the taxpayer who must sue the IRS for overpaid taxes. This long and costly battle is only pursued by those people who have legitimate claims. The IRS programs its computers to flag these big or repetitious items for its agents to examine more closely. It is the greedy person who gets caught on this type of deduction.

-- *Charity* – While charity begins at home, the potential for abuse has grown as the IRS tightens other deductions. While the maximum allowed charitable expense allowed is 30percent of gross income, the higher the tax bracket, a well thought out "gift" is money in the bank.

Jack, a Texan, has large oil royalties. He was looking for a way to reduce his tax bill. On a trip to New York, he made the rounds of a number of used book stores buying first editions of any books he could find. Most of them were of unknown authors, though he managed to buy some first editions of recognized authors. With the help of his accountant, Jack donated ten books from his "first edition collection" to the local university each year and claimed the charitable deduction. One hundred dollars to a local book shop owner insured Jack that in any conflict with the IRS he had substantiation as to the value of the books. The first time Jack's return was questioned, Jack presented the revenue agent with the written valuation of the collection from the book store owner. The deduction was allowed, and Jack continued to make his charitable contributions each year.

This ploy of donating to charity works well for other valuables where the price varies according to the buyer. The price of art, antiques, collectibles, jewelry and furs fluctuates with the economy. Buying items wholesale and donating them to a local charity at retail pricing is a common ploy which the IRS has been trying to eliminate for years. Recent record prices for gold and silver have made these items quite valuable as write off, especially if Aunt Millie's sterling silver set was inherited but never recorded.

For the simple fibber, out of pocket donations to the church, girl scouts or university can be inflated by hundreds of percent. However, the IRS now requires documentation of the weekly church offering before it will allow the deduction.

MAIL ORDER MINISTRIES

The tensions between church and state have always been focused on the power of the purse. The Founding Fathers protected religion from government taxation under the First Amendment guarantee of freedom of religion. In the 1960's, churches became a refuge for some long suffering taxpayers.

The Universal Life Church has ordained over twenty million ministers by mail and issued 50,000 church charters since the 1960s. By numbers alone, this significant move to religion caused concern at the IRS. The agency counterattacked with new rules and regulations. But the taxpayer who becomes a minister still has a strong footing.

In one case, in response to tax exemptions granted by the government to some fringe religious groups, four towns in upstate New York staged a mini tax rebellion by its entire citizen becoming members of the Universal Life Church and turning their homes into churches thus exempting them from property taxes.

The major advantage of this tax set-up is the charity deduction. By donating most of his salary to the church and using church owner property (house, car, boat) the individual avoids a major portion of taxation. The International Congress of Churches & Ministers can provide an umbrella to set up an exempt ministry that complies with the IRS rules for churches at no charge.

The IRS test for the validity of the church is whether the church is organized and operated exclusively in furtherance of its avowed religious purpose. And the tax courts have ruled that the court could not consider the merits or fallacies of any religion which effectively permits any group to operate a church.

Another great advantage of church membership is the allowances for missionary work. Members soon dispense with vacations and spend their time doing missionary work in Las Vegas, Florida or Hawaii and other areas that need their ministries. Naturally, the church pays for the entire trip.

Though tax officials have mounted a counter attack against these "church schemes" to avoid taxes, the First Amendment privilege greatly limits the ground rules for the IRS. Since the content of the religion is beyond question, the test becomes organizational. With more sophistication of the new preachers of the gospel of the "hereafter," these churches are thwarting what the government is here after – taxes.

TAX SHELTERS

With the enormous bite taxes take from every level of income, especially of the upper middle class, tax shelters spring up as fast as the IRS can shut them down. The rhetoric of some politicians that a couple is wealthy in New York or California if they make a joint of income of $200,000 is ludicrous.

There are some legal ways to save on taxes: oil and gas depreciation, cattle, historic buildings, and other favored items. But the rules on these shelters change from one Congress to the next and always flag the return by the IRS computers. Audits are more likely if the taxpayer attempts to offset ordinary income with tax shelter losses. These options should only be considered with a good accountant and competent tax attorney.

Feeling beleaguered by the number of sharp attorneys and tax professionals, the IRS tried to push through a rule that would bar any attorney or CPA from practice before the tax court if he has engaged in a disallowed tax shelter plan. Naturally, the IRS refuses to list approved plans in advance of the investment by an individual. The agency enjoys the safety of hindsight by putting the entire burden of proof on the shoulders of the public. "They should have known better" is the reasoning on retroactive rulings.

The vehemence of the IRS attacks on shelter is characterized by costly litigation. Taxpayers, right or wrong, are subjected to the bureaucratic insistence that there is something tainted about shelters and must be abolished. Even when Congress permits certain types of sheltered income, the IRS inevitably rules as narrowly as possible to permit as few taxpayers as possible from taking advantage of the law.

Law groups continue to fight the encroachment on the attorney/client privilege. But these efforts are only temporary setbacks for the governments that need to continue to find revenue to feed its spending programs. And all this is done in the name of people who "voluntarily" pay taxes.

A LITTLE WHITE LIE

While the government lends lip service to the idea that the "cheaters" are hurting all honest taxpayers, the reverse might actually be true. Most of the IRS models come from the statistical models of what is normal for any given tax bracket in any given location. When the total population of the country begins to inch deductions up to compensate for bracket creep and the devalued dollar, the models of compliance automatically permit a higher degree of cheating.

Because of the internal pressure on tax agents to "bring in cash," the IRS concentrates on larger and more profitable cases rather than on the average guy case. Guidelines for agents require that no felony prosecution be considered unless he has not paid $5,000 in taxes for the past three years. That means a married person making $50,000 could file no income tax return and not risk criminal prosecution.

This type of incentive, though meant as an administrative expedient, penalizes the "Honest Abe" and rewards the "Dastardly Dan." The irrational approach of the tax man is often dictated by the laws Congress passes which further destroy the individual incentive to comply. While paying more than required in taxes is never rewarded, honest mistakes can often be the beginning of a long battle with the government.

Penalties on thrift and profit from wise investments are beginning to be recognized as disincentives to hard work. A penny saved this year which earns interest for a rainy day is taxed as ordinary income tomorrow. But if you borrow too much money on a mortgage you can't afford, you can deduct the interest and get government assistance to get you out of foreclosure.

Why sacrifice today to buy next week? Why tell the government that you possess the old fashion virtues of diligence, thrift and honesty?

The notion of voluntary compliance with the tax system is more a public relations gambit by government than a realistic appraisal about how Americans feel about the taxes they pay and how the government spends the money it receives.

VI

CACHE

"Collecting more taxes than is absolutely necessary is legalized robbery"

Calvin Coolidge

Business deals tend to be very private affairs, usually carried out by people with mutual respect and trust. Shady deals are more private. The myth that private affairs should or can be public knowledge is absurd. While we have the campaign laws that force officials to make public the records of all donations, no one is going to report the $50,000 cash bribe. The money given under the table is hidden from everyone but a few, unless the givers turn out to be FBI agents.

People who are in business casually conduct side business. With a certain sophistication of being paid for work, deals among neighbors, friends, acquaintances, business associates transpire every day. Small businesses operating in volume and cash offer the perfect temptation, high gain—low risk, to every person. Appealing to honesty in the name of government is a forced and phony ignorance of family and individual needs. The conservative trend in America has its roots in the inability of government to spend money wisely coupled with a liberal belief that all social problems - are solvable with money.

Without choosing political philosophy, "cache" business is motivated by personal gain, pure and simple. This simple philosophy leads the small businessman as well as the corporate chief to manipulate dollars to show less than maximum taxable income. As with all of the underground economy, the opportunities are so numerous that no government can ever control these transactions.

SKIMMING

As soon as the income tax passed, the small merchant began taking a little off the top. Any owner-operated retail operation provides limitless opportunities for keeping part of the take. The simplicity of the act, hidden among the day-to-day struggles of owning and running a small business, increases the palatability of the action to most people. Daily losses from breakage, theft, vandalism and carelessness are incentives which push strong people over the line. The drawer full of cash is perhaps the most irresistible temptation. "Just for this pair of shoes, just for dinner tonight, just for the kids' Little League uniform"- there are endless reasons and justifications for taking the money you earned for your life before the government spends it on some study of why convicts want to escape from jail.

George owns a restaurant which has a small bar attached to it in Portland, Maine. Buying it six years ago took all the savings he had made during fifteen years in the Navy and a second mortgage on his house. The beautiful brick warehouse along the waterfront had potential.

For two years, George, his wife Gwen and two of his children worked restoring a warm feeling to the two rooms. It was just the right combination for those cold New England nights. During the first year, the used refrigeration units died costing George nearly $6000. The banks wouldn't loan the money to him, the Government wouldn't loan it to him. With too much of his life invested to call it quits, George cashed in his life insurance, and a small policy he bought out of basic training. They sold the twenty foot daysailer he bought when he retired and they borrowed some money from a loan shark George knew from his Navy days.

The hours became gruelingly long when they opened for breakfast at six just to earn the extra $100. It paid the day's electric bill eighteen hours a day became routine for both of them, beginning at five o'clock shopping for vegetables. They were open to 1 am, the legal closing time. George pulled the night shift, Gwen the morning.

Three years later downtown began to undergo a revival. More merchants renovated buildings encouraging a thriving night life. Overnight his business changed into a success. Breakfast was cut out except for Sunday brunch and bills were paid to suppliers in 30 days not 60 to 90 days. And George began dipping into the till.

At first it was for petty cash items, like gas, home booze and incidental personal items like ammunition during hunting season. The trick was always simple, when a customer paid in cash and George was running the register, he'd make change but not ring up the sale. Too simple to pass up, he thought. Life had been passing him by, making him work without the little enjoyments. Now he and Gwen would begin to live a little. Gwen learned the same habit, using the money to buy things for the house and the kids.

After two years they were hit with an IRS audit and the experience put all of their business efforts into a narrow frame. Within minutes of sitting down with the agent, George knew he was in for trouble.

The special agent, ever so polite, grilled George on his business expenses, especially the automobile and liquor. He cut both deductions in half. Then the agent went after his travel and entertainment deduction, disallowing everything that George didn't have a receipt for and even some of the ones for which he did have documents and collateral material. Angry, frightened, George waited for the agent to cull his receipts to find all the money which had been skimmed from the business. But the agent was satisfied with the hefty $5000 increase in George's taxes and never got into that part of the business.

When the agent left, George realized that it was safer to skim from register than to try and get deductions by the IRS. That set the pattern of business for Gwen and George. Using two sets of books, they began a systematic looting of their own business, showing little increase in sales from year to year. He began paying some suppliers in cash for certain deliveries of liquor, meat and produce. Though business audits have come with some frequency, the accounting method shows a healthy profit which satisfies the agent who can assess more taxes.

Skimming from the register takes place in many small owner operated business. The fear of these proprietors is that employees might help themselves to the same type of dipping. Though universal product codes and computer controlled inventories make it easier for the IRS to catch some types of retail establishments, it is a hit or miss operation. According to George, the trick to not getting caught is 'don't be greedy." A business which shows little book profits while enlarging the restaurant will automatically raise the suspicion of the taxmen.

KICK BACKS

A common practice in lining pockets is the kickback, an ancient and revered method of paying the middle man or supplier for business while enriching the payor. It is a payment by a supplier for business which might go to a competitor. Sometimes kickbacks go to middle level employees of a firm who, by their control of purchasing power, can direct huge amounts of business in the direction of favored suppliers. Other times, it is merely a way to conceal income on the books of a company by raising the expenses on a project in order to reduce the taxable profits. The Chinese have for centuries recognized it as "the hidden hand."

Tom has been a building materials dealer in Houston since it was a hot construction market. In the business for ten years, he had developed some close business dealings with several of the medium size developers—builders in the community. But as the city grew, the competition for customers grew fierce.

Billy Ray, a longtime customer and builder/developer in Houston came to Tom with a simple deal. On all orders from BR Construction, twenty percent worth of materials would be added and charged per job. Billy Ray pays Tom with no questions asked and passes the higher "cost" onto the buyer or building owner. Tom splits the higher billing with Billy Ray and still has the material (already accounted for on the books as having been bought) to sell for cash to other contractors.

With everyone making money, Tom began the same kickback practice with a few other developers to the tune of $20,000 a month. Billy Ray was in turn giving kickback money to zoning commission members to approve density requirements in restricted areas. All of these side deals were easily concealed in the complex building transactions. And as long as no one became unhappy with the arrangements, the network keeps money in everyone's pocket.

In certain industries, kickbacks are almost institutionalized. Trucking, real estate, shipping, movies, construction, etc. have unwritten rules which heavily depend upon "consulting" fees. American firms from Lockheed to Halliburton realize that foreign business contracts often cannot be obtained without gratuities to develop a climate "favorable for business." While there are laws prohibiting these types of arrangements, the reality comes down to a simple choice; do business or don't do business. Kickbacks can be disguised in a multitude of skins and a variety of colors, but the basic idea remains - a piece of the action.

A variation on the kickback theme is payment for non-existent goods or services. This tack works when the purchasing agent or procurement officer knows that he is being billed on non-delivered goods. After okaying payment on these fictional goods, the agent receives his share of the money. Officials in the Government Services Administration (GSA) have been found guilty of hundreds of thousand dollars' worth of false billing. One painting firm was paid for painting the same building five times in one year.

Military items, especially those items which are difficult to inventory like food and clothing, are often subject to the same sleazy payment plans. The ordinance officer with control over this area or his sergeant is the likely accomplices with the supplier.

The massive government programs especially Medicare and Medicaid introduced a new set of opportunities for underground operators. The size of these programs and the reliance on the integrity of the doctors has provided many cracks for cash to fall through. The billing from false laboratories, for services not performed or for unneeded surgery is routinely approved by the paying agencies. With such temptation, millions of dollars are siphoned into crime controlled laboratories or through phony clinics.

BRIBERY

Bribery, of course, is illegal. No government can sustain its legitimacy if its officials tolerate the open taking of money in exchange for the performance of official duties (though some countries in the world do operate this way.) But governments, being composed of men and women, are susceptible to the enticements of the flesh. Though the United States is not a corrupt nation by the world's standards, we do have pockets of corruption.

Government contracts, local, state or Federal, offer the biggest prizes and greatest opportunity for human failings. One person often decides these contracts, usually worth millions of dollars. While the contract formally must be bid upon, more often than not, the decision is made on reputation, contacts and money.

The big cases such as Alan Hevesi, controller of New York, or Congressmen Duke Cunningham or Representative Charlie Rangel (who as chairman of the House Ways and Means Committee writes tax law) didn't know what taxable income was received nationwide attention. It is not the people in the high places who have the most opportunity. The local Commissioner of Public Works, Building Inspector, Zoning Board, and Licensing Board has much more leeway and flexibility to engage in petty corruption.

The Chicago Tribune, to test how easy it was to uncover corruption in Chicago, opened a bar in an elaborate attempt to expose citywide corruption. Immediately the health inspectors, building inspectors and liquor authority inspectors arrived to do their job. But they let it be known that for a bit of cash they could overlook infractions (real and imagined). These public servants swarmed out of the woodwork like so many resident cockroaches. For low bribes of $20 to $50 a month they would prevent problems from arising in compliance with city ordinances. Naturally the ordinances were complicated enough that almost anyone was guilty of something at any time. With remarkable gall, these petty officials paraded a litany of advice on who to bribe, how much and the advantages the tavern owners would receive for taking care of the right people.

Not surprisingly, the city took action against the officials, the newspaper created publicity and sold papers and the petty corruption resumed business as usual after hoopla died down. Honesty is a relative term in the field of commerce. Bribery is often initiated by the owner, who because he is not in compliance with a city building ordinance offers the official money to overlook the infraction. And the official, feeling like a good guy, does the owner a favor by accepting the money and allowing the law to be bent.

It is not only government officials who receive or solicit bribes. The larger number is in the private sectors in return for the sizeable business contracts which are under discussion. Purchasing agents, buyers and procurement officers are in the best positions to benefit from this commercial game of give and take.

Fredrick is the purchasing agent for a West Coast toy chain of eight stores with a yearly sales figure of $80,000,000. When he orders his Christmas merchandise, his decision usually determines the year for any number of small toy manufacturers. As savvy business people, the manufacturers have developed a relationship with Freddy. It costs them an additional $50,000 a year in "production costs" and Freddy has walking-around money for most of the year.

Recession years are good for Freddy because the cost of his decision increases inversely with the depth of the recession. That is, the more they need the business, the more valuable his decision. But the equilibrium of give and take keeps his greed in line when a manufacturer has a hot line, Freddy needs an inside track to get the toys before his competitors, so he may kickback some of the profits to the manufacturer rep or salesman. It makes business interesting year after year.

Fortune 500 companies like Ashland Oil, Bethlehem Steel, Firestone, Goodyear, Gulf, Phillips Petroleum, and Joseph Seagram have been convicted of bribery. The surprising thing is that they were caught. At the international corporate level, money is nearly impossible to trace.

Clifford Wise was the head of Bethlehem Steel's ship repair sales office in New York. In Switzerland, a company named Office pour le Financement du Commerce et de l'Idustrie (OFOI) was the laundry firm for Bethlehem's cash. OFCI had a world-wide network of agents who sold ship repair services.

Wise would attach a sales commission to repair work being done at one of the Bethlehem's yards and pay this money to OFCI. After it had entered OFCI books, it was ready for American use. OFCI first took its 30percent commission for the use of its facilities. How did Wise get the money back to the United States? Simple, he or his secretary would fly on the corporate jet to Switzerland on business, fill a briefcase with cash and return. The money was then used for normal round of bribery and kickbacks. Millions of dollars passed through his hands over the years without ever being detected in the legitimate economy.

Gulf Oil used a subsidiary in Nassau to launder money tagged for oil exploration back into the U.S. to be used as handouts to various friends. Firestone Tire & Rubber Co. went even further concealing nearly $2.6 billion in a special reserve accounts which were never reported. The money was deposited by the Chief Financial Officer who oversaw distribution for the good of the company and himself. In 1979 the company pleaded guilty to two counts of income tax evasion, but the money had joined the underground river of cash, used for those purposes of reward and consumption. These examples only demonstrate the ease which large amounts of cash appear and disappear from the approved, counted economy.

Since 1980 United States corporations have been found guilty of transferring over $1 billion into the shadow areas of the economy by illegal methods. This represents a small fraction of the true total which occurs every working day. There is virtually nothing the American government can do to police multi-national corporations aside from the hit or miss, slap on the wrist, prosecution which happen in rare cases. The universe is too large for the government to detect the movements of each dollar. What is remarkable about American business is that despite the enormous opportunity for bribery, cheating and kickbacks, not that much takes place. In comparison to businesses in other countries, American business is honest.

FARM INCOME

Farmers, as the backbone of America, enjoy a nostalgic and romantic place in the American mind. Cognizant of the political implications, farmers also enjoy tax advantage. The IRS estimates that farmers do not report 30 percent of their income but independent estimates put the figure higher or about $50 billion per year.

Most of this non-reporting is easily hidden from view in the myriad of expenses which the ordinary farmer (and corporate farmers) is allowed as well as the favorable situation for mixing personal and business expenses. And there is no way anyone can keep an accurate tab on how much grain or produce is raised on any farm because the numbers are too large. Since the beginning of taxation, farmers have found ways to avoid their "master's" taxes.

The conservative nature of farmers and the traditional values that prefer cash to credit, trade to purchase and privacy to public knowledge reinforce the tendency to avoid the legally prescribed tax dictates. And the benign neglect of enforcement by the IRS allows the avoidance behavior to flourish.

But farmers also enjoy a legislative benefit that normal business people do not have. Because of a belief in 1915 that farmers were not sophisticated enough to use accrual accounting, farmers were permitted cash accounting. This advantage is rigorously defended by farm groups despite the modern management techniques and increased mechanization of the farm. At the same time, government price supports, development aid, subsidies for ethanol and other farm subsidies put farmers in a favored position on receiving government assistance.

Cash accounting favors the farmer in major ways. Expenses such as farm equipment and machinery can be deducted as current expenses while an ordinary business would have to write-off the cost of the machinery over its useful life as depreciation. This line deduction means immediate return of current dollars rather than keeping the money tied up in capital goods.

Selling livestock is treated as capital gains rather than the less favorable straight income. Keeping breeding animals of any kind, even for personal use, is encouraged because each calf is money in the bank.

Improvements on land and crops allow farmers enormous room to maneuver for tax deductions. Since the accounting system permits them as current deductions, in a good year, a farmer comes up with acres of land he had cleared, terraced, fertilized, graded or otherwise improved.

Since IRS auditors are not farmers, they have no way of knowing if a certain field really was improved, or for that matter whether the improvement took place this year or last. Unable to quantify in the normal accountant's linear fashion and not encouraged by IRS regulations or supervisors, agents allow farmers greater latitude in claiming business expenses for running the farm.

Jeremy is a fourth generation farmer in Wabash, Indiana. His 200 acre farm is mixed use between soybeans and corn both of which have been excellent crops in recent years. While Jeremy and his family are staunch Republican Hoosiers, they regularly and aggressively avoid taxes because they know they can. To a certain extent, they would be fools if they didn't take advantage of the opportunities provided by legislation and lax enforcement.

This year, Jeremy bought a new Ford pickup with a full sound system, air conditioning, and steel-belted radial tires. He listed it under farm equipment and deducted the entire cost from current receipts. He usually buys a new truck every two years. His wife and both sons drive the old pickups which were also written off as farm equipment.

By law, only that portion of the truck which is being used for business purposes should be deducted, but since no one has ever challenged the deduction, Jeremy takes it on every piece of equipment. They even allowed a snowmobile when he said he needed it to check his fields in the winter.

Mixing business with personal needs is a way of life around the farm. Last year, while repairing a leaky roof on the barn, Jeremy reroofed the house as well. Total cost, $18,000 but he deducted the entire bill from farm income. Most normal repairs and routine maintenance around the house use farm materials saving the Wilson's thousands of dollars every year. The normal taxpaying family is treated severely by the IRS if they mix business and personal expenses.

Barter, too, is an accepted method of transaction down on the farm. Jeremy and his neighbors swap animals for seed grain, fertilizers, labor and machinery. No records are kept of the transactions, and the country boys know better than to volunteer information to the revenue agent. Local farm bureau agents advise them on new legitimate deductions which they can take for casualty loss from insects, storms, drought and snow. In 2009, Indiana farmers received over $25 million in government payments while benefiting, from the liberal tax laws and enforcement procedures.

Finally, the actual production of corn and soybeans can never be counted by any revenue agent. Part of each year's harvest is put aside and sold for cash during the year to different grain merchants. No farmer likes to bring his entire crops to market at the same time. Commodity prices are important to the delivery date, so Jeremy like any smart farmer tries to sell when the price is advantageous. Sometimes he forgets to put the transaction into his account ledger.

The holes in the system are numerous with deliberate thanks to the strong political power of the agricultural lobby. As the tax laws were written each year, the farmers managed exclusion of it because the system is too complicated for the unsophisticated country folks. But the "Big Business" of farming was granted a dispensation from the rules which apply to everyone else. But like everyone else, farmers bend and break those rules for personal profit.

HIDE AND SEEK

Few people put their money in an iron box, dig a hole under a distinguishable landmark in a deserted place and cover it up to retrieve at a later date. The Captain Kidd method of tax evasion hasn't been popular for years. Yet the treasure map to many American fortunes leads the IRS to some fairly remote outposts.

Not every country follows the lead of Washington in demanding to know about every banking transaction over $5,000. Foreign bank accounts must be reported by law to the Internal Revenue Service, but many people simply overlook this requirement. Even in a complete audit, unless a person deposits or sends a check from his usual bank to his foreign account, it is virtually impossible for government agents to check.

Foreign bankers are less than cooperative with authorities unless the investigation is a large scale criminal matter. While some countries do cooperate with American tax officials, for the most part, they could care less about the results of a tax probe. These facts disturb the enforcers of the tax laws. By using propaganda, the IRS gives the public the impression that foreign accounts are accessible to their scrutiny. By publicizing cases where someone is caught or by going after celebrities, the IRS maximizes its public relations effort at little expense to the agency. The gullible public believes the press releases while sophisticated tax shelter lawyers advise their clients to open accounts in the Bahamas, Cayman Islands, Switzerland, Singapore, Hong Kong or Liechtenstein. The Swiss banks have come under increased pressure by revenue pressed governments in Europe and the U.S. They have made some gestures of cooperation but there are still many bastions of secrecy in the Alps.

Hard pressed government agents must stoop to crime (breaking and entering, theft, purchasing stole computer records) in order to obtain information on the banking activities of American citizens in foreign countries. Recent pressure on some of the major Swiss banks has eroded some of the secrecy of those accounts. By using selective prosecution and amnesty programs, the government coaxed a number of individuals to voluntarily pay avoided taxes with penalties but avoid any criminal charges. United States court permitted illegally obtained documents, stolen from a bank official in the Bahamas, as evidence for tax court purposes. Are not tax officials bound by the criminal codes?

Foreign accounts in the Bahamas and Cayman Islands have become big business because of the tax policies of Western, industrial nations. People don't go through the trouble, time and expense of keeping an account in the Cayman Islands because they need a local bank to cash a check during their vacation. Tax policies cause capital to flee. This law of economics was evident in the Middle Ages.

While safety of these accounts is not generally questioned, the accessibility of the money tends to make them more of a hassle than a bargain. Unless the taxpayer is of sufficient wealth to keep part of his money hidden thousands of miles away, the gambit is not very useful. But the IRS found the Bahamas, because of their close proximity to Florida (30 minutes by air), the major off-shore concern. The eruption of drug money in Florida convinced IRS that millions of taxable dollars were hiding in the banks on the islands. While the IRS is no doubt correct, the money is hidden because it cannot be declared. Again, the dilemma of the underground economy.

Domestic banks offer a variation of the hidden account to every customer in the form of the safe deposit box. These boxes across the country probably hold more cash than most major banks. And they are of great use to every member of the underground economy.

Though used for storing valuables like jewelry, titles, wills and other items of value, safe deposit boxes are one of the few places large amounts of cash are stored without raising any eyebrows. Being a smart agency, the IRS provides a deduction for the box on the return. Any taxpayer who takes this generous deduction of a few dollars also provides the IRS with the exact location of any hidden cash.

While most people think the IRS can't get into a safe deposit box without a warrant that is a far cry from the truth of the situation. Many times by just flashing his badge to the bank manager, an agent can gain access to a box. Though not as common as in past years, if you are under criminal investigation, few of the rules apply. Generally, the safe deposit box is where millions of underground dollars lay each day, earning no interest, invested in no companies but paying no taxes.

A myriad of small investments, hard to trace, have gained acceptance as ways to avoid some tax bite. Uncle Sam even issues some of them. Treasury notes, certificates of deposit, bonds which have been paying different yields can generally be bought without the IRS being notified. If the taxpayer doesn't declare the proceeds, it is extremely difficult for the IRS to trace unless it is with the single broker who handles other financial investments.

Investors who know their way around the stock market find that capital gains can be hidden. Brokerage houses, especially on the international scene, do not report every trade to the IRS as some people think. In fact, many firms will not deliver records of a client's transactions without a court order. What the government does receive in a list of dividends paid to each account the IRS can't judge a person's stock investments from that information.

Many stocks however do not pay dividends. These are usually new issues, over-the-counter or small exchange stocks. Though there are some New York Stock Exchange companies which pay no dividends. To hide these profits, investors an open account with a broker to handle only non-dividend stocks. As soon as a stock begins to pay dividends, it must be sold or the account becomes visible to the IRS. That does not mean the tax man will find it, but the record exists. This type of game is tough to control and usually is done by those sophisticated in the equity markets.

VII

THE HARD WAY

"Smuggling, black markets, illegal transactions of all kinds are every bit as ubiquitous as taxes, undermining all respect for the law, yet performing a valuable social service by offsetting to some extent the rigidity of central planning and making it possible for needs to be satisfied."

Milton Friedman, Free to Choose

Since Al Capone's bust for tax evasion in 1929, Americans have assumed that the criminal world is closely scrutinized by the Internal Revenue Service. But this myth is more a public relations gesture for the service rather than the reality of life.

Treasury estimates of money gained from criminal activities is $160 billion per year. This includes the old time favorites of gambling and prostitution and the new big money item, drugs. But it doesn't include white collar crimes like embezzlement, fraud and investment schemes or burglary, theft, racketeering, or elaborate Ponzi schemes like Bernie Madoff.

In this Pro League, the players can become fabulously rich in a relatively short period of time. And the money which they garner is funneled into the legal economy in various ways. This *"washing"* of cash allow these underground players to bring money into the legal light while protecting it for their old age.

The Tax Reform Act of 1976, passed in response to the Nixon misuse of the IRS as a political tool, has eliminated much of the cooperation between the IRS and other law enforcement agencies. If the present rules existed when Capone was around, the IRS would never have prosecuted him.

To protect the agency from criticism, IRS lawyers maintain a rigid interpretation to the law which forbids the disclosure of tax information. The IRS has effectively cut out the cooperation with the

FBI or DEA except under tightly controlled court orders. While these rules may have made a joint law enforcement attack on illegal income more difficult, the magnitude of the problem defies an easy solution. There are not enough cops to contend with the relaxing standards of American society.

Increasing acceptance of marijuana and cocaine use, gambling and prostitution place law enforcement officials at odds with the communities they are trying to protect. Cooperation from the public is more difficult to obtain and voluntary information is hard to come by. Like catching water in a sieve, the few people who are apprehended do not impact the overall situation.

Hard figures on illegal income are impossible to obtain because of the nature of the operations. Drugs, primarily marijuana, accounts for $48 billion, with gambling at $14 billion and prostitution around $20 billion. The government loses approximately $15 billion in taxes. One Senate sub-committee calculated illegal income at $160 billion with $40 billion lost in taxes. In either case, the figures are staggering.

Enforcement problems are compounded by criminals who do not file income tax returns. This hides them in an enormous pool of poor, uneducated Americans who do not file each year. The IRS spends only a tiny percentage of its funds and manpower searching for non-filers preferring to concentrate on auditing returns which have been filed.

With a little tax advice from a lawyer or an accountant, the big time criminal minimizes his chances of going to jail. By filing returns and declaring some of his income in categories which fit into the IRS norms of taxpayer compliance, he no longer is in technical violation. Then, if he is caught, the charge is underreporting rather than criminal fraud. By playing hide and seek with the government, the savvy operator covers most bases without disrupting his flow of cash.

POT POWER

Smoking pot which gained wide acceptance in the hippie movement of the 1960's and developed into a form of protest against the

79

Vietnam War and traditional middle class lifestyles, is now as American as apple pie. Twelve states have decriminalized pot and one, Alaska, legalized private use and cultivation. California has recently proposed a statewide referendum to legalize and tax pot to help solve its budget crisis. Medical marijuana exemptions have sprouted around the country like so many cannabis weeds.

The Department of Health Education and Welfare estimates that over 43 million Americans have smoked pot with 20 million using it regularly. Total cigarette sales are $88 billion; liquor, beer and wine sales are $120 billion, while pot sales are $40-48 billion according to the Drug Enforcement Agency estimate.

Some officials believe that 150,000 to 200,000 people make their living from the industry. This puts pot in the same league as Exxon and General Electric.

From the big time smuggler who brings Mother Ship (generally an old freighter, either unregistered or with foreign registration under a flag of convenience) up the coast of the United States carrying tons of pot from Columbia to the 17 year old kid from Brooklyn who sells loose joints for a buck a piece behind the Public Library in New York City, the profit on each sale or "turn" of the weed is a tremendous incentive. Any supermarket manager, salesman, or marketing manager would salivate at the profit margin and rate of return of this industry. Because of the risk factor, the only obstacle to conventional business operations, a 100percent return on investment, every two to six months is reasonable to expect.

The arithmetic is simple. If you begin with $10,000 and turn it once every two months, in one year you will make $320,000 in cash. The growth is geometric. If you stay in business for five years, you retire for life. With the government collecting NO taxes on profit it's the last way to be the overnight American tycoon - the last Carnegie or Rockefeller before the passage of the 16th amendment. Without income tax, the person who takes the risk keeps the profit.

With returns like this, and the individualistic character of Americans, hundreds of thousands of ambitious, hungry, and talented people find the pot trade a good living. Flyers, sailors, truckers - men who take chances with the elements, find the lure of big money too tempting to resist. And though some go to jail, the majority makes big money, in cash.

Tommy and Jimmy grew up together in South Philadelphia and were as close as brothers. After college, Tommy, a skinny kid with a trace of acne, began managing one of his father's dress shops. But he wanted his *own* business and soon opened a small used car lot. Jimmy moved to Atlantic City to sell catering goods to the hotels. Dissatisfied with the tiny commission on trays, forks and spoons, he became a representative for nearly twenty different lines.

They kept in touch and with their business knowledge began building a pot empire. The first year it was small deals, 50 lbs. and 100 lbs. to old neighborhood friends. Then the numbers began getting big. Jimmy made the buys, Tommy the sales. With their first sale of a ton for $400,000 to the owner of a refuse disposal company, they knew they had it made. Incredulously, they saw their boyhood dreams of fortune being realized.

Most of the pot was sold to old friends from the neighborhood and a few friends from the business world. They became partners in the used car business as a cover for their real livelihoods. They were grossing a million dollars a year before they were thirty. Deciding to go into the big time, they moved to Miami, the Wall Street of the drug trade. They opened a used car lot as well as a string of satellite corporations to conceal their dealings. With their domestic distribution set, they expanded vertically and went into the import business.

After briefly tussling with the Cuban syndicates who run a large portion of the Miami drug trade, Jimmy and Tommy set up connections in Columbia. Soon they were shipping 3000 lbs. a week to Philadelphia and their distribution network. Both of them bought million dollar houses on the beach. Their wives dressed in diamonds and designer originals. With fleets of cars and corporate jets, they were enjoying the good life.

Both Tommy and Jimmy filed corporate tax returns laundering part of their cash through the corporation. No one counts how many cars actually come in or out of a used lot. Faking invoices, receipts and expenses like any other business; they brought part of the money into the legal economy. And they filed personal income taxes, declaring money from their profitable business. All they did was underestimate their actual incomes by several million a year. And there was no way the government could detect it.

By this time they were importing pot with throw-away yachts which were used once or twice then scuttled at sea. $70,000 cash buys any number of ships with owners only too happy to sell for cash to someone they would never see again. Capital gains were quick and hidden.

The old DC-3 planes with a hired pilot and co-pilot for $60,000 for the three hour flight were left on the dirt runways after the cargo was unloaded. But the profits kept rolling in, with little concern for the above-ground commercial life. Tommy and Jimmy rented an office with a billiard table, grand piano, second floor bedroom, all looking out across the brilliant blue ocean and sky. High above the Gold Coast of Florida, the two boys from Philly had nothing better to do with their money than have gold plumbing fixtures in the bathrooms.

But for these two, the dream did not last. Drug Enforcement and FBI agents put a criminal racketeering and smuggling case together against the two which resulted in long prison sentences. But the IRS never got to win any of the back taxes on this operation which was estimated to gross over $500 million a year.

DEA admits that despite the size of this operation, it certainly wasn't the largest in existence nor did putting it out of business seriously dent the marijuana industry. While importers and smugglers have been the focus of most media attention, a large and profitable sector of the pot industry is literally growing around the country. Smuggling has inherent risks which domestic cultivation does not have. And who are the best farmers in the world? Americans. And who has time to check millions of acres of crops for a few hundred rows of pot? No one.

In California, pot is now the number one cash crop in that rich agricultural state, winning out over the grape by a nip. Mendocino, Sonoma, Humboldt and the more northern reaches of the state produce high quality sinsemilla worth over $1000 an ounce. The agricultural commissioner of Mendocino Country listed marijuana as the county's leading crop in his 1979 report valued at $90 million. It is much larger today.

Kentucky, once the largest producer of pot (hemp) for ropes during the Second World War, has been presented with a marijuana feasibility study to set up a state monopoly, patterned on the ones that run the alcohol and tobacco industries. This agency would bag the pot as loose tobacco, label it for potency, and tax it with the use of an official tax stamp. Already cultivation is widespread in Kentucky, Tennessee, California, Florida, Hawaii and regions in the South and Midwest. Even conservative farmers understand a cash crop which they can make money on. It is estimated that pot is top cash crop in 12 states and one of the top three crops in 30 states.

Andy and Jean were renting a small farm outside of Paris, Kentucky. He is the regional salesman for a coal company headquartered in Pikesville, Ky. His sales are mostly to small utilities and some of the smaller businesses and schools which still burn coal for fuel. His wife teaches second grade at one of the local schools. They were born and raised in Indiana from strong church going families. And they attend their Methodist church each Sunday.

One winter, Andy's brother gave him a bag of marijuana seeds which he had saved for years. That spring, when Andy planted his annual garden, he added rows of marijuana between his rows of corn. Though they worried a lot that first year, the September harvest was worth the wait. Harvesting nearly 200 lbs., they earned $86,000 cash that summer. In two years, the farm was paid off and they had options of two other places near them.

The work is difficult, especially grooming the plants so that they bring a better price. But since that first year, they haven't worried about the police. No one comes out that far into the country unless they are asked. Private property is respected. If pot were legalized, Andy thinks he would become a full-time farmer. He doesn't understand why tobacco is legal even though it is a proven killer, while pot is illegal. As he and many of his grower friends see it, the government could collect more taxes from pot than from either liquor or tobacco because the unit price is higher. He is content as a small time supplier to his limited network of recreational users.

Andy's right about the tax part of the economic equation. While it costs Andy up to $50/lb. to raise, his selling price is from to $500 to $2000 per pound. Again, most of the mark-up is due to the risk factor. If the government added an excise tax and sales tax, some economists predict $10-40 billion could be collected by the government without raising the street price of pot.

Since the Treasury Department already has a bureaucracy, the Alcohol, Tobacco and Firearms, which could collect the tax and monitor the industry, the question is political rather than economic or practical.

Though the government spends nearly $40 billion a year trying to enforce pot laws, the industry grows larger and more sophisticated. Set up like a legitimate business with manufacturer, importer, wholesaler and retailer, tax compliance would increase down the line if more people could declare both business and corporate profits.

Marijuana is a thriving multi-billion dollar industry that is forbidden to pay taxes. It is a consumer of tax dollars when it could be a significant source of tax income. The pot industry is the largest single underground business in the United States. With nearly 25 percent of the population, from retirees to college kids smoking pot, only legalization and government regulation can hope to discover the true size of the industry and bring the money into the legal economy. Until that time, hundreds of thousands of Americans and billions of dollars must remain in the underground economy.

The political pressure to keep pot illegal continues to erode as politicians from the President through scores of legislators, judges and other establishment figure have admitted to having used the forbidden weed at some point in their lives. The enormous financial pressures that the Federal and State governments face may be making the most persuasive case to look at the legalization and taxation of this agriculture crop. Not only would the tax collection increase dramatically but the cost of law enforcement would fall.

CLASSY COKE

The sister to the marijuana trade, and once the most socially chic drug, is cocaine. Once it was the specialty drug of the beautiful people. But like other pleasant substances, the middle class cultivated a taste for it. Young professionals coming into their prime earning years, buy coke for that party or weekend get-together.

The phenomenon cuts a wide path through all of the Sun Belt cities as well as the big cities of the East and West coasts. Finding cocaine isn't difficult; finding good cocaine is.

Cash money is the propelling force in this trade as well. The profits are enormous; the product is in demand; the markup is 200 to 500 percent; and the social life is great.

Since law enforcement attempts at suppression have been less than successful. Many of the dealers, traders, importers and lawyers are, in fact, engaged in the same professions above ground.

These people understand the law and their professions enough to conceal the wealth and to make the paper trail difficult to follow. There are some big players, but the game is filled with small and medium size ambitious, educated hustlers. Cocaine is not a drug for the poor. It is the "crème de la crème" of the drug world and costs over $80-120 per gram depending on quality. The people who use coke possess the savoir faire to outwit, or at least, disguise the trail so that the IRS has little opportunity to crack down on this form of income.

Cocaine is worth between $38 billion in annual sales, more income than any retail chain earns. And no taxes are paid or collected.

Randall was born to moderately successful parents in Memphis, and grew up as a church goer, little leaguer, and paper boy.

After graduating from the University of Tennessee, he moved to Denver to get an architectural degree. His wife, Gerry, went to school in California receiving a degree in urban planning.

They met in Denver at a party of young professionals. Those first years were lean, business-wise for them, but they began making a good living from the cocaine trade. She had the connection in California who imported the white powder; Randy sold some of it in Denver to other guys at the gym. He also flew back to Tennessee to deliver pounds to his old fraternity brothers, most of who were in the business world.

The first year they earned over $50,000 in cash from the cocaine business. Most of the money was thrown away on the good life - skiing, clothes, cars, entertainment and such. Then business began to boom.

Randy gave up the idea of architecture and went into a cash business, opening a restaurant in Glendale. He was selling more than a kilo (2.2 pounds) a month and couldn't supply the demand. The money was rolling in. Gerry, a polished, articulate woman, was working for the regional transportation authority and finding customers among her colleagues and social acquaintances.

In three years, they had a ski lodge in Steamboat, a house on Lake Tahoe, a boat, four cars, and a new house. With their two regular incomes, and the restaurant, Randy laundered $300,000 a year through his legal circles. The rest of the cash was used to buy jewelry, or kept in liquid assets in an account in the Cayman Islands.

Randy often repeats the story to friends of how Coca-Cola got its start as the good feeling soft drink. Cocaine was a widely used beverage additive until it was banned in 1914 by the Harrison Act. He also uses Sigmund Freud and Arthur Conan Doyle in his conversations in defense of his right to trade in an illegal product.

The economics are simple. There is a huge demand for cocaine from the society. The supplies are limited, the risks are high but the profits are enormous. Once the coke is through customs, it never stays around long enough for the police to have any chance of finding it. Cocaine is done in the privacy of many good homes.

A kilo costs Randy $80,000. By cutting it to make seven pounds, each selling for $25,000, Randy makes $95,000 on one deal. If he wants to be greedy, he can sell to the next level (by the ounce) and net another $40,000 on each pound. And so on down to the people who buy grams. The original cost of the kilo of cocaine in Columbia or Peru is around $12,000. Knowing that the government cannot eradicate its use, Randy feels he might as well profit from the market.

Randy and Gerry's story is repeated thousands of times by doctors, lawyers, accountants, businessmen, celebrities and athletes. Coke runs in the best circles, among the cream of American professionals from the White House down. And though there are some high profile arrests, the law does little to deter its use. The rewards greatly outweigh the risks.

GAMBLING

Gambling has undergone a profound political rethinking in the last thirty years as state politicians across the country have discovered this form of taxation. Casinos, racetracks, Jai-alai, and lotteries have proliferated as this form of "voluntary" taxation was rediscovered.

Gambling, like alcohol and sex, has been found in most societies throughout the history of man. The joys and pains of gambling cannot be replaced or prohibited. From the foot of the Cross to the Irish sweepstakes, the thrill of beating the odds strokes the ego and dispels the depression of the day. And there is always hope because there is always another day at the races.

This voluntary taxation, as gambling is euphemistically called, has undergone a complete reversal of perception in America. Forty years ago it was a crime to possess a lottery ticket, of any kind, in most states. When New Hampshire introduced its lottery in 1964, many neighboring states enforced their laws by arresting citizens who bought the lottery tickets.

But the success of New Hampshire in raising money spurred the more pragmatic states to recognize gambling's existence as well as its profit potential. Under the guise of helping to fund education, New York State instituted a state lottery which now includes daily numbers, football bets, super bonus jackpots, and million dollar grand prizes and a multimillion dollar advertising budget encouraging people to play.

While state governments continue to search for "risk free" taxation, the cost of government enforcement escalates. This in turn, has become a weighty factor in political decisions because any government spending eventually costs the taxpayer. And with public sentiment strongly against raising taxes, judicious politicians look for other means of revenue. When the suppression of an industry like gambling can be transformed into a cash spigot, it is the moralists not the pragmatists who object.

New York State has become a case study in government entry into the "gaming business." With the widest variety of legal outlets, New York has set up head-to-head competition with organized crime in the daily, weekly and monthly lotteries. As in any other business enterprise, the government is attempting through advertising and attractive prizes, to break traditional buying (betting) habits of the population. Through off-track betting parlors, and various fans of the numbers games, this strategy of competition has been the most successful program in reducing criminal income from gambling. The activity of betting has not decreased. The money is only being redirected. Casino gambling, once as exotic as bottled water, became a major growth industry in America. However, with the explosion of Indian casinos, riverboat casinos and other variations, the easy money is gone.

But the problem remains for the legislature. Where one cash business exists, others soon follow. In Atlantic City, as in Nevada, prostitution, drugs and assorted schemers have congregated. Bribery of government officials, skimming from receipts, laundering of other illegal money, infiltration by organized crime begins. And this worries the good citizens who are not involved and do not have a piece of the action, and the reasoning come full circle to prohibition which does not work.

In Nevada, long pointed to as the epitome of legalized gambling, the games of chance provide 45 percent of the state 2008 revenue. Gross gambling revenues for Nevada in 2008 were $11 billion dollars. Total gaming revenue in the US in 2007 was $92.3 billion. The money king capability of gambling is not in question.

Rather the perfidy of the act (throwing away the family paycheck on a roll of the dice) will always trouble politicians and other social critics. The larger good of societal equilibrium, balancing the desires of the population with the "reasonable" assessment of the public good, dictates that gambling should be a government run business rather than a crime. The relaxation of legal attitudes toward gambling may have spurred rather than hindered the growth of the underground sector.

Calvin is broad shouldered and 6'2", 230 lbs. He was too slow to make the football team at University of Texas. But his interest in football and sports intensified once his active career was over. Every weekend, before a game, Cal would run the football pool for the fraternity, with the Longhorns usually being the heavy favorites. Cal devised point spreads to increase his volume and his winnings. The closer the season came to an end, the more frantic the betting became and the greater thrill Cal got every time his home team beat the point spread.

By his senior year, Cal's business was thriving. Every Tuesday he had football sheets printed with the weekly games on them, both college and professional. For two dollars, anyone could pick winners with the point spread. The catch was they had to be right on five games. Cal was bringing in over $3,000 a week during the regular season and over $5,000 during the bowl weeks at the end of the season.

Graduation didn't dent his business; rather it gave him time to pursue his occupation full time. He was running his betting parlor year round with football, basketball, hockey, baseball, and even soccer as lucrative betting sectors. His modis operandi was the betting sheet which he distributed each Monday and picked-up each Friday. He had six girls working for him in his office in Austin, and opened branches in Houston and Dallas, keeping in touch with many of his ex-classmates.

Cal with his hearty laugh and wide Texas smile was a big time bookmaker by the age of 26, handling ten million dollars in bets each year. He had some overhead, such as secretaries and telephone lines. He computerized his regulars and provided them online access to his sheets with payments through PayPal. Living in the high style, Cal was taking home between ten and twenty thousand dollars a week - more in the football season than in the slow baseball season. Ninety percent of his customers were college graduates who were working full time in Texas. The twenty or fifty dollars a week they would bet at Cal's simply substituted for the bet they might have placed in the local tavern with one of the guys. Though it didn't stop them from placing another bet there as well.

Cal believes he is providing a service to people who want it and can afford it. With the national "line" on TV each weekend and even the local sports writers speculating on the point spread, Cal feels justified. If he could do it legally and above board, he would. But since it is underground, he feels no desire to change the status quo because his profits are enormous and all tax free. With almost the archetypical Texas bravado, he declares, 'No slimy political bastard can tell a Texan when he can or can't place a bet on his football team. It's unpatriotic."

The scene is repeated in every city in the country, from Miami to Minneapolis. Sports bettors are mostly male, with varied degrees of education. In offices, taverns and suburban dens, sports are a national passion.

According to the IRS, bookmaking handles over S41 billion in bets each year with nearly all of the money remaining in the illegal sector. In fact $2.5 billion is illegally wagered on the Super Bowl alone. Cal has never, filed an income tax form yet grosses over $500,000 a year. While bookmaking by people from the middle class, like Cal, is not unusual, in most big cities, this lucrative operation is controlled by organized crime elements. Boston, Buffalo, Philadelphia, Cleveland, Baltimore, Detroit, New York all have well-organized bookmaking operations which are remarkably honest, returning nearly 60 percent of the wagers to bettors in the form of winnings.

New online gambling forums continue to spring up as fast as the government can try to identify and close them. Often with off-shore locations for their servers, individuals can bet on a variety of games, using off shore PayPal or other types of accounts. The current estimates of the online gambling take from the United States alone is $5.4 billion

While American officials are beginning to realize that gambling is a voluntary human activity which has endured for centuries, governments of Asia, Africa and Latin America have been financing most of their operations out of the proceeds from lotteries. Even the American Revolution, was for the most part, financed by lotteries and raffles conducted by Gouverneur Morris and others in regular colonial lotteries. With the current tax revolution forcing politicians into creative financing, there is nothing like reinventing the wheel to increase tax collections.

SEXY PROFITS

Unlike gambling or marijuana, there is no talk in the United States of legalizing the world's oldest profession, prostitution. Though the sexual revolution and the feminist movement have greatly changed our perception of sex for sale, the gut level reaction in the country is overwhelmingly opposed to prostitution.

While prostitution is legal in England, Germany, Canada, Netherlands and other European countries, the United States is still unwilling to address it. Amsterdam has run its famous "red light" district for years with girls advertising in windows but they are subject to regular health inspections.

In most major cities, a woman is as close as the phone or the internet. Listed in the on the internet under Erotic Services or in Yellow Pages under escort service or massage parlor, with only a phone call, a woman will come to your hotel or home for any service desired. In the larger cities, the services provide men as well. What's more, these services accept Master Charge, Visa or American

Express. Often they will give business vouchers or receipts for corporate customers who want to submit the bill with their expense accounts. Brothels operate discreetly in most cities. Posing as health clubs, massage parlors or simply hidden in a residential or commercial neighborhood, they provide a service to the community.

With the explosion of the internet, individuals can meet each other online – out of the sight of any law enforcement officials, to do business between consenting adults. The popular website Craigslist, offered Erotic Services, for and among consenting adults. How many people were participating or how much money has been exchanged is subject to the imagination. It was only a murder of a call girl by a deranged medical student who she met on the web site that led prosecutors to call for the shutdown of the Craigslist service.

But did the end of Craigslist service end the online sexual bazaar? Not a chance, the business simply migrates elsewhere. There are chat rooms, bulletin boards, local recommendations and specific websites of adult service providers detailing what they will do and how much it will cost. Girls can work for an agency that can handle bookings and security or she can go out on her own with a website, e-mail and cell phone. Such services as Adultfinder.com provides a simple search site to unite buyers and sellers. The sophisticated call girl can earn between $2,500 and $10,000 a week.

When the governor of New York, Elliot Spitzer (Client 9), wanted a girl, he arranged for a service to deliver her to his hotel where he was traveling and he provided a wire transfer to cover the service. The problem with Mr. Spitzer's arrangement was he left a trail that any rookie law enforcement officer (he was a former attorney general) could follow. Cash, however, tells few tales.

Because sex for money is so common in America, the IRS has little way of estimating the actual size of the industry. Conservative estimates of $20 billion yearly for the sex trade is extrapolated from police arrest records bearing little reality to the numerous call girl services.

HOT STUFF

Crime is certainly not a new way to make money. It is always hidden from governmental scrutiny. It's difficult to estimate the true size of this segment of society. But anything that can be sold can be stolen.

The thriving market in stolen merchandise is estimated at $ 10-14 billion a year. Any goods from automobiles and electronics to gasoline and steaks can be "fenced" in the criminal world. These goods usually are sold into the legitimate sector of the economy. While many of these goods result in net losses, the use of insurance and tax write-offs in casualty loss turns part of this business into a sophisticated racket to help ailing companies. Simple scams like return fraud where shoplifted items are returned for cash or receipts for higher purchase price are simple.

A new twist in stolen goods has developed in recent years, counterfeiting. Clothing labels, especially high priced designer jeans, have developed another avenue for making a buck underground. Off shore or domestic companies knock off the design of a high line product, produce realistic labels and sell their products through stores, flea markets and gray market outlets. While many consumers can suspect that the goods are a fraud, the price and the prestige make them too attractive to refuse. Identity thefts and thefts of credit cards and credit card numbers has burgeoned with the wide spread use of online purchasing. Organized rings of thieves turned electronic impulses into hard goods and cash that are being charged to an unsuspecting person's account. And the thieves will continue to be inventive and opportunistic where crime is concerned.

Loan sharking, a mainstay of organized crime, garners nearly one billion dollars a year in interest. Running these underground banks has always been a relatively safe method for racketeers to increase their capital with little risk. Charging a typical 100percent interest on a loan per two weeks, a $100 debt becomes $400 in a matter of a month. Since big guys with lots of muscle generally are the ones doing the collecting, there are few arguments about the terms of repayment.

Arson for hire, cigarette smuggling from state to state, fireworks, firearms, immigration papers and literally hundreds of other scams are buried in the darkest corners of the subterranean economy. Each of these items look to take advantage of natural arbitrage bringing products from places they are unrestricted or taxed at a lower rate to states where they are highly restricted or highly taxed. It is simply a good business proposition for those who are willing to undertake the risk of arrest.

BLACK AND WHITE MARKETS

No government has ever been successful in suppressing the desires of its population for available goods. Despite penalties like death or life imprisonment, individuals are willing to take the risk for the economic gain if the market is there.

Massive tax evasion is the only course open to smugglers and peddlers, gamblers and hookers. By forcing consumption of desired objects underground through political fiat, based on moral prejudice, politicians created the Pro League of tax evaders. Instead of raising $50 to $100 billion in revenues by taxing these activities, the government spends billions attempting to enforce the unenforceable, throwing good money after bad.

Nearly 40 percent of the population is participating in the black market, underground economy. Disorganized, with no program to push, no candidate willing to speak for them, the underground economy is downplayed in importance. And in political terms, it is powerless! But in real, economic terms, the shortsighted political interests are driving a greater percentage of the population outside the law, clearly a frightening trend.

Special interest groups have become the dominant weed on the Hill in Washington. Politicians, never known for intellectual fortitude, increase the burden on the average citizen through taxes and inflation to satisfy well-oiled lobbying efforts. The citizen with little chance of changing the legislation opts out of the system by joining the underground economy.

In the cases of marijuana and gambling, large minorities are driven into breaking the law, resulting in diminished respect for other laws as well. Tax laws are rapidly joining the growing lists of laws which many citizens are choosing to ignore. Through various means, the individual avoids the unpleasant aspects of his action while trying to increase the pleasant ones.

This market is also a significant backstop to the economy when recession hits and people are laid off from above ground jobs. By relying on their wits and entrepreneurial spirit, Americans can cut out their Uncle Sam and work to put bread on their tables and keep their dignity and self-respect in tack.

The black market is thriving because politicians, motivated by self-interest, find these moral issues easy to rail against, without encountering any organized political opposition. But the problem is now serious with less than 40percent of the eligible voters participating in the electoral process. The underground, black market products fill a need, expressed by the American people, voting with their pocketbooks.

VIII
STRAIGHT TIME

"The only difference between a taxman and a taxidermist is that the taxidermist leaves the skin."

Mark Twain

Working Americans, getting by at a survival level, often with two or three jobs don't pay taxes if the money isn't withheld from their pay checks. Small employers, with marginally successful businesses, are only too willing to avoid the expense, time and confusion of filing forms. Minimum wage, or less with tips, quite often is the rule, but without taxes it means more.

Straight time earners are the maids, cab drivers, laundry ladies, gardeners, waitresses, handymen, part-time admins, receptionists, baby sitters, nannies, seamstresses, and all types of temporary help. They are the people who work to stay alive, working longer to meet their needs. The economic truth about the straight timers is they exist just over the poverty line yet are full of the pride which hopes for a better life. The full burden of taxes if they paid them (they pay sales and excise taxes on alcohol, tobacco and gasoline) would push many of these people into poverty. No one avoids taxes in the United States, the question is always how much tax and who should be paying it.

Straight timers are the ordinary people, the ones who put in their time, effort and much of their lives to make enough money to stay ahead. They are the ones who perform service jobs, menial jobs, second jobs, part-time jobs, night-time jobs. Straight timers are usually lowly paid, minimum wage or under and often rely on tips for a major portion of their income.

Tax law complexities are ignored at this level of society because the rules and regulations are so much gibberish to these people. There is no sophistication about ripping off the government or undermining the national interest. Straight timers are for the most part, simple people trying to get by. Wealthy or talented people do not spend their time at minimum wage rates; it makes no economic sense. Skilled craftspeople who add value to their products don't have to sell their time at straight wages. Straight timers are the working poor who aspire for a better way of life.

Undocumented and illegal immigrants – mainly Hispanic – who labor in domestic jobs like cleaning houses, working as nannies or in the labor areas from construction to gardening - work to support themselves and their families. They hope that their children can benefit from the American dream just as previous waves of immigrants have. They cannot pay income tax because to do so would put their immigration status at risk of exposure and potentially subject them to deportation. As non-citizens, they can't obtain a social security card which eliminates legal employment. Though many have forged or used other people's social security card, illegal immigrants, for the most part, try to stay below the government radar.

When the original income tax was passed, people who fell into the lowest income categories were not expected to pay any taxes. They were not expected to file any forms with the government or be part of some huge government database. The framers assumed that meeting the basic needs of food, shelter, clothing and education would consume all of their income. Lowering exemptions during World War II and inflation makes nearly everyone libel for some taxes, if only FICA. With the current minimum tax rate beginning at $8,025, a person can work full time at $7.25/hour. or about $60 a day and owe taxes. The same person may qualify, however, for food stamps, earned income credits, energy credits and even welfare in some states. People who earn $15,000 or less have roughly 10 percent of their income taxed away by the Federal government (in FICA and Medicare taxes), to pay for many social programs which may want to give the money back to them at enormous costs to every taxpayer. They pay a greater portion of their income in other taxes on gasoline, cigarettes, imports, alcohol as well state and local sales taxes. Straight timers have to avoid taxes in order to make it.

CITY HUSTLERS

Cities are always difficult places to survive. Action and work are needed to stay even in the fast paced economic jungle of urban America. And cities, because of their size, are places where the surplus theory of labor still exists. Getting and keeping good jobs are still real challenges.

Yet in a highly concentrated collection of people, service industries abound. Waiters, bartenders, maids, domestics, cab drivers, delivery men, peddlers and thousands of other professions offer personal service to specific individuals for a limited period of time. Cash is the easiest, and usually the only way, to pay for these services.

Mary is a waitress at the Glass Saloon, a local restaurant, in St. Louis. Divorced with one child, she works five days a week, 4 to 9:30 pm. A high school graduate, she dropped out of junior college when she was twenty to get married. Now 27, she supports herself and her daughter on the $600 a week she takes home. Her hourly pay is $3.25 but her tips are over $70 a night on Friday and Saturdays. Three days a week, she works at an unlicensed day care center and is paid off the books.

When her husband left, Mary was completely lost. Originally from Pittsburgh, she had no family to turn to, not that they would have been much help. Having never held a job, she was completely lost and was forced to apply for welfare. After six months of that, the degradation of sitting in the welfare office listening to women wallow in their handouts, Mary felt the ebbing of self-respect and began searching the want ads. Her waitressing career began on the 4 to 12 shift at the Dunkin Donuts located off I-70. Mary is ignorant about most tax laws. She doesn't file any income tax returns, and never has. Believing that the withholding taxes her employer deducts from her $3.25 wages cover her tax liabilities. Mary figures that the government already has the money why bother with tax forms she doesn't understand. She's not malicious in her tax avoidance, and would probably pay taxes if anyone came and asked her for them. Under the present system, figuring out how much she owes and whether she would make ends meet if she pays more taxes cancels her motivation to comply with the law. With the new law now withholding taxes on any tips paid with credit cards, she asks her customers not to leave the tip on the credit card but in cash. Most are very willing to comply.

Dymtro doesn't pay income taxes for another reason; he can't afford them. An immigrant from the Ukraine, Dymtro came to the United States in the early 1980's and began driving a cab in Washington, D.C. Though he was a dentist in his native country, his knowledge of English is too limited for him ever to hope to practice here. A legal immigrant, he works seven days a week to earn the money to bring the rest of his family to the United States. Driven by the old immigrant desire for a better future, Dymtro wants his children to be educated in the United States.

When he arrived, he was alone. After three years, he had saved enough money to bring his wife and two of his children to join him. Now he wants his parents and his brother's family to come. Humble about his abilities, Dymtro wants to be a good American. He hustles to make a living from the tips, working most of the tough hours in the evenings, generally twelve hour shifts. His ambition is to own his own taxi and to learn to read English well. Until that time, he is preoccupied with his personal quest of supporting his family here and in the old country.

He learned the system of not declaring any tips from the other cabbies in the garage. To them, tips are a matter of personal service. No one has to give a tip. A guy's entitled to the money he earns and besides, no one ever knows how much you bring in each night. While not totally naive, Dymtro accepts that what he is doing is correct by American standards.

In the big cities, small time entrepreneurs of all types hustle for a living, breaking many of the rules of "proper" business by not filing the necessary paperwork. There work is so transitory that complying with the red tape would negate the profitable activity.

Jackie once worked on Seventh Avenue, in the fashion district, as a racker of women's clothing. After fighting with several bosses, Jackie split rather than take the abuse. He didn't quit the fashion world; rather he brought it to the street with hundreds of other sidewalk peddlers.

From his years in the garment district, Jackie knew where to get seconds, irregulars and overstock items. He also can get limited first issues at wholesale prices. With a movable display rack, Jackie sets up in the morning by the subway stop coming in from Queens to entice the ladies on their way to work. At lunch time, he is usually in the Fifties on Third Avenue where the women greedily handle his dresses, blouses, skirts and belts. Since he carries no overhead, he sells 100 to 200percent lower than the merchants around him. At five, he wheels his display back to 42nd St. to try and sell the remainder to the ladies on their way home.

Jackie doesn't work every day. Mondays and Tuesdays are too slow, unless the date is the first or fifteenth of the month, traditional paydays. Fridays are always good because the girls like something pretty for the weekends. The work is easy in good weather, but the trick is to make it through the winter. Gloves, hats, scarves and sweaters become his staple items during the cold season, but he figures he drinks five times as much coffee to keep from freezing. Yearly income ranges between $25,000 and $40,000 for Jackie depending on the weather, the lines he picks up, and the number of times he gets hassled in periodic "crackdowns" by the city police on unlicensed peddlers.

Having never graduated high school, Jackie is very pleased with his status as an independent businessman. He is married; he gets to spend mornings and long weekends with his two children. He doesn't think much about the future, nor does he believe that he will ever retire. On those cold winter days, he wishes he owned his own shop but the thought of all the paperwork banishes the idea as soon as the good weather arrives. He hopes his kids stay in school and get good jobs with vacations and benefits when they grow up.

Tough economic times destroy any budget. More dual income families exist now than ever in our country and the number is on the increase. Low paying part time jobs, off the books, often offer women with children the most convenient job. Since they are usually covered under their husband's medical and insurance plans, cash employment makes economic sense for both parties. The dollar earned is the dollar paid. It helps with food money, and the little extras of life.

Second jobs, traditionally held by men, continue to be important to families. Young men with growing families and burning ambition have often worked twenty hours a day to get ahead in life. These second jobs are progressively becoming underground ways of making a living.

Tom was an Oakland city fireman. With fifteen years on the force, he had regular hours, pulling the day shift. For eight years, he had a second job to support his wife and three children. Recent years have gotten very tough since Tom, a very traditional Italian, refuses to allow his wife to work.

Having worked traditional second jobs with the appropriate taxes being withheld, Tom jumped at the chance to work as the weekend bartender at a place opened by a retired fireman. At first, Tom felt some guilt about not paying taxes and the chance he might be caught by the IRS. But his friend assured him that there was no way the government could find out even if they audited the bar. Reluctant at first, Tom took the extra money figuring that, at the worst, the IRS would make him pay taxes on the money later. But the pressing problems of his growing family were more important. After seven years off the books, Tom retired from the fire department and bought a bar and lounge himself. Now he employs a fellow fireman as a part time bartender, off the books.

Janice also took a job in order to help her family meet the bills. Thirty-five, married and the mother of three children, Janice had no intentions of working. Though she was a licensed practical nurse, she gave up the career goals willingly to become a full time mother.

Her husband Gerry, a short barrel chested delivery driver, was happy with the relationship because he felt his children should have a full time mother. But when his distributor closed, Gerry was out of work with little prospect of a new job. Unemployment and union benefits helped for a while but the family was falling behind. Gerry tried to find work, but handyman jobs were all he could find.

Janice dusted off her license and began looking after patients during the day; two days a week became five days soon after she started. The money wasn't great, about $400 a week, but she was always paid in cash. Neither of them ever thought to declare the income because they didn't have enough to raise their kids. Gerry wants to pay taxes again, but he wants work.

Their dilemma is resolved in favor of economic survival rather than in favor of a government whose economic policies (causing unemployment) have caused their dreams to be wrecked. But Gerry was also collecting unemployment insurance for the first twenty-six weeks he was laid off and was happy when it was extended. He managed a few odd jobs, he didn't report the fact that he worked to the government. Thus he was violating the unemployment law as do millions of other people every year.

No issue angers the average taxpayer more than the tale of the welfare cheat who picks up welfare checks in a Cadillac. Though there are cases, to be sure, in which this happens, the overwhelming amount of cheating on government payments occurs by people who do some part time work while receiving assistance.

These people who receive welfare, unemployment, food stamps and social security benefits are generally aware that working or concealing assets is strictly against the rules. They know they are cheating the system. But poverty justifies the excesses.

Jennette is an 81 year old widow who worked as a sales lady in a small women's shop in her native North Carolina town until she was 75. Age began to affect her movements and she was forced to quit. Her husband, who had died thirty years before left little in the way of a pension so Jennette was forced to live on social security of about $1,200 a month. Though she qualified for food stamps, she was too proud to ask for charity.

She had, however, one thousand shares of General Electric which her husband had bought for $2 a share. The quarterly dividend check helped her along, but she never even thought that she should tell the government about the money. And, though she couldn't walk well, her crocheting was still adept. The shop she used to work for sold whatever she produced, about $1,200 a year. With these few items, Jennette managed to get along until she died. She stopped filing income tax forms when she retired.

Sidney is twenty years old. His father died when he was ten, so he was receiving Supplemental Security Income. After high school, he began junior college and continued to receive the money. But college didn't last and he dropped out and began working as a pizza delivery man. He collected SSI payments until he was twenty-one.

The Social Security Administration estimates that about 3 percent of its payments or roughly $275 million were paid in ineligible or excessive payments. This underground money which is never declared in taxes because it falls on the poverty side of the Internal Revenue enforcement guidelines continues to buy goods and services in the legal economy.

While Social Security, especially SSI payments, has a high potential for abuse, unemployment compensation is the most widely used form of supplemental income to people working in the underground economy. Seasonal workers like carpenters, gardeners and vacation employees work their necessary twenty six weeks and then collect benefits the other twenty six weeks. Enforcement is so lax and the system is so overworked that if the employer doesn't contest the claim, the person receives the $405 per week.

Ken is an actor who lives in New York City. Not very successful, he generally gets work in summer stock in the small towns in Upstate New York and Pennsylvania. He manages to keep working for the required number of weeks after which he is qualified to collect his check. During his off season, when he is studying acting and looking for parts, he works as a driver for a limousine service making nearly $300 a night for a night on the town. He would never think of reporting the money and the overworked unemployment office cannot possibly check up on him. He was tremendously pleased when the President extended benefits to 99 weeks because it meant he would not have to work for a year, if he did not want to.

Welfare, which is predominantly collected by women with young children, is also a base level upon which underground work flourishes. These women, while collecting their monthly check can work as maids, laundry help, babysitters and a host of off the books types of jobs. Motivation, not opportunity, is the major ingredient to success in this field. Since earned income penalizes the worker by reducing welfare, the incentive is to lie about work.

Since the founding of the United States, the newest immigrants are always the most exploited class of people. Forced into low paying jobs with little security, arriving from countries where opportunities and expectations were much lower, they are ripe for the unscrupulous employer. The present situation in this country, where most immigrants live with the fear of exposure and deportation, the employer holds even more cards. The worker is afraid to complain or demand. He is willing to work for less than minimum wage with no fringe benefits or taxes taken from his salary.

Jesus traveled to the United States from Guadalajara three years ago as a seasonal fruit picker for the farmers of the Central Valley in California. When the season was over, he found work in a cannery in the suburbs of Los Angeles where he worked for $4.50 per hour. The cannery is a small one owned by an American citizen of Mexican descent who exploited his countrymen with low wages, but relied on the illegal labor to keep his plant competitive with the other, larger operations.

Jesus is only 24 and lives in a two room apartment in the Los Angeles barrio with four other young men from his village. They send nearly half of their pay home to their families yet consider themselves lucky to be working in the United States. In a year Jesus hopes to return home and visit, but he wants to live in the United States because his life is much better here. But he lives in fear of the immigration officials so he demands very little at work, trying to be content with the few opportunities life has provided him. He dreams about bringing his wife and children to live with him in Los Angeles.

Kathleen is also an illegal immigrant who came to Boston on a tourist visa from Ireland and never returned. The first year she worked as a waitress in a sleazy old men's Irish bar in South Boston.

Kathleen wanted to come to America for years but the legal immigration quotas were filled. Her friend Meagan had gone two years before and was happy and about to be married. Then she would be an American citizen. The first job was easy to get; Kathleen slept with the manager. Since that time, she got a social security number in a false name, but prefers cash waitressing. A bit plump and a plain faced colleen, she works in a nicer Irish pub downtown, three days a week.

She is mostly over most of her terror of being deported but she lives with a morbid guilt for having entered the country illegally. Meagan told her that getting married solved her guilt problems. Kathleen hopes it does, but in the meantime she is working two jobs and learning without the complications of taxes.

ILLEGAL ALIENS

Over 12 million people contribute to the gross national product of the country by producing goods and services at a lower cost. Domestics in New York, Houston, and Los Angeles are only possible because of the illegal Latin populations. The garment district in New York, the canneries of the West Coast, and labor jobs throughout the country are filled by people who want to work. America provides that opportunity. But the fear of deportation keeps these illegals from paying (except by consumption taxes) for the services of the country. However, in order to work illegal immigrants must use a social security number. According to the Social Security Administration, illegal aliens pay $7 billion a year in social security taxes which they will never collect.

Like the generations before, these immigrants are not becoming rich. Mostly they are laying the ground so that their children will live better. The reason for immigrating to the United States is still the same - "tomorrow promises to be better than today."

MARGINAL EXISTENCE

As long as man has existed, there has been inequality in economic life. Those on the lowest rung, with the fewest skills and resources, make a living by any method available. The modern social democracies (including the U.S.) have seen fit to provide a floor under which no one theoretically can slip.

But the poverty line is elusive, cost of living varies and many reasons exist why people prefer to stay out of the eyes of the state. While tax laws may apply to this economic class because of the expansion of the taxing power of the central government, much of the taxed money is returned to the same class through transfer payments.

Taxes on income less than $15,000 a year amounts to the government charging a handling fee for providing the same income to the same class of people. Straight timers can only earn money by putting in the labor. The framers of the income tax never expected this working poor to have to deal with the sophisticated notions of accounting. But wars and social programs have changed the agendas of legislators. Everyone possible should pay taxes. The government can decide who gets the money back through other programs.

The IRS takes this into account when it looks over unfiled returns. Poor people tend to fall through the cracks of the system by moving with no forwarding address or failing to file for several years. In many cases, the IRS could owe refunds if returns were filed. Educating this portion of society to their financial and tax obligations, bookkeeping obligations and deductions seems like an impossible task. Since there is no formal tax instruction in any of our secondary schools (which have a hard time teaching arithmetic) there is no effort to convey this information.

Working on a very cost conscious basis, the IRS knows that the amount of taxes it could possibly collect would be outweighed by the cost of information and collection. Straight timers are the in the giant sea of taxpayers who just aren't worth the trouble to pursue.

IX

DEFENSE

"Anyone may so arrange his affairs that his taxes shall be as low as possible. He is not bound to choose that pattern which will best pay the government."

Judge Learned Hand

Honesty is no defense against the Internal Revenue Service. God-fearing clean living, patriotic Americans have as much chance for the fearsome TCMP (Taxpayer Compliance Measurement Program) audit as does the street shyster. Why? Because the IRS believes that everyone lies or cheats on his taxes. Or if the cheating isn't deliberate, the taxes could be calculated more in favor of the government. The basic rule of the IRS is when in doubt, disallow the deduction.

While most people believe that they are innocent until proven guilty, anyone experienced with the tax man knows that the opposite is the case. And the TCMP is the nightmare everyone dreams about. Every two years the IRS selects roughly 40,000 returns from every tax category (as selected by the IRS computer) to grill. *You* don't have to do anything to get on this list and you can do nothing to avoid it. Good, bad or ugly, if the IRS wants you, there is no choice about it. And no reason is offered or given why any individual is so lucky.

The premise of the TCMP is that Americans underpay their taxes. TCMP audits are used (according to agency) to figure the amount of cheating which is taking place. From their data, the IRS feels it can determine how much cheating to let the individual get away with and how much is normal.

The TCMP reveals to the government more about the personal life of an individual than any police investigation can. When the audit begins, the agent requires that the taxpayer prove every item on the return, from his name and social security number, to his marriage certificate and the birth certificates of his children. All checks, bank accounts, bills, medical records, employment records and any other material pertaining to the spending of your income may be required without a warrant. This grilling can take days of your time even if the taxpayer has overpaid his taxes for years, no refunds will result.

At the end of the session, the taxpayer's life is recorded on computers and tucked into government files only to be closed after the IRS takes its share of the estate when the taxpayer dies.

Naturally, the IRS would like the manpower to conduct this type of investigation of every tax return. Since they can't, they target individual groups or persons for audits of particular items on a return. They also have an elaborate system of weighing line items to increase odds of the ordinary audit. Independent contractors and professionals are more likely to be audited than salaried employees, higher income people more likely than lower, high deductions rather than low deductions.

Tax audits are, through the courtesy of the IRS, a dreaded event. In some cases, the audit or threat of an audit has caused heart attacks, strokes and death. But when the audit strikes, underground players have the most to lose. IRS penalties can be severe, with long prison terms as the ultimate sentence.

THE PENALTY BOX

Getting caught breaking the rules of the game can cost the underground citizen everything. While going to jail sounds like the worst thing that could happen, when the government seizes all property and bank accounts, an upper middle class family can be turned into instant paupers. To collect taxes owed the government; the IRS has a number of weapons at its disposal.

-- *Liens* - After auditing a person's tax return, if a balance is due, the IRS can slap a lien on any real property a taxpayer owns. It can attach a car, boat, house, business, as well as the rights to property. Only by satisfying the taxes, can the taxpayer regain his property. In 2008, the IRS filed 500,000 liens.

-- *Levies* - The IRS also has the right to attach property which the taxpayer has given to a third party for safe keeping. This simply means, the IRS can take any bank accounts, stocks, or wages a person possesses. There is little a taxpayer can do because the IRS generally attaches accounts without notice. Based upon the idea that the taxpayer might move the money, in 2007, the IRS filed 3.7 million levies according to the National Taxpayer Advocate 2008 Annual Report.

-- *Seizure* - While the 4th Amendment to the constitution prohibits the government from unreasonable search and seizure, the 16th Amendment has been interpreted to permit the IRS to seize taxpayer's assets for non-payment of taxes. This can occur with purely administrative actions and does not necessarily involve any court case. Appeals and court remedies may come after the fact (discussed later) but the taxpayer is without use of his property during the proceedings. The IRS is not required to obtain market value for any property seized. So a $500,000 home might be sold for $200,000 just to satisfy the taxpayer's obligation. In 2007 the IRS reported 676 seizures.

"Sovereign's Stranglehold" sounds like a grip used by Henry VIII. But it is a variation on seizure which tickles the fancy of some IRS agents. Officially, Federal taxes are payable once a year but the IRS can force an individual to pay immediately. The taxpayers left to wrestle in its (sovereign's stranglehold) grip are at a stark disadvantage. The taxpayer may be rendered indigent overnight, but the government's position has to be protected.

Jeopardy assessment is another variation on seizure. In addition to any back taxes a person may owe, the IRS may seek a jeopardy assessment to be added to the taxes already owed. This assessment is usually used to confiscate all wealth immediately and without prior notice. It almost always exceeds a taxpayer's net worth. One man owed $300,000 in back taxes. The IRS assigned a jeopardy assessment of $3 million and seized all his assets in order to protect the government's position.

-- *Prison* - The ultimate penalty the government can impose on a citizen for not paying taxes is prison. While this Damoclean sword is poised over every taxpayer, only 2,200 people were sent to jail in 2008 on tax related charges. The IRS prefers to take the money rather than be involved in a criminal prosecution that will be time consuming, expensive and where the rules of the game change in favor of the individual. Rules of evidence, self-incrimination, and probable cause all serve to protect the individual from unjustified intrusion into his personal life. The IRS likes having the information and prefers to try tax cases in tax courts, with a tax judge and no jury.

While these are the extreme punishments which the government can administer, these are the least likely forms of punishment. Greater vengeance is better dealt in the medium of the crime, money. Most players in the underground economy only draw light penalties plus interest on the unpaid balance. For the most part, the IRS has given up hope of stopping the small time operator. It can't be justified in time, money or results. It's the professional player where the best catches lie.

DISPUTING THE CALL

The first rule in any dispute with the government is "keep your mouth shut!" In an audit, or any criminal investigation, the individual does more harm than good by needless speech. When the IRS comes to the door, they are only interested in one thing - leaving with more money. They already believe you have cheated on your taxes and a few indiscriminate remarks will point them in the right direction.

The accountant and lawyer are the first line of defense for anyone dealing with the government. There are several ways to contest an IRS ruling which assesses more taxes. Fighting the agency, however, is both expensive and time consuming. It can also lead to continuous audits during the litigation process. But many people do take up the challenge.

In tax cases, there are two ways to fight. The first way permits you not to pay the tax and appeal the rulings; the other way forces you to pay the tax and then file for a refund. There are advantages and disadvantages to both.

-- *Tax Court* - is the place the Internal Revenue wants to settle most claims. The court, with jurisdictions over most cases, is made up of judges who know the tax law, its interpretations and precedents. To encourage taxpayers to use the tax court, the IRS allows the taxpayer to use his money until the case is settled. The taxpayer is not required to pay all taxes and penalties before going to court.

The tax judge hears the dispute without a jury resolving primarily factual evidence in the case. Generally a tax judge is only guided by the application of settled legal principles. That is, the tax judge applies the IRS rules to the facts of a specific case. The IRS is represented by the Chief Counsel's office of the Treasury Department.

Complicated tax decisions such as tax cases involving corporations or estates are usually handled in tax court because the application of the convoluted tax decisions can only be applied by judges familiar with the territory. In tax court, the IRS is on home field knowing which judges make what kind of decisions. They also know all the fine points of the process. Unfavorable opinions may be appealed to the Court of Appeals.

-- *District Court* operates on traditional trial rules with which most Americans are familiar. The taxpayer may request a jury trial which will, in turn, determine the facts of the case. Here the taxpayer has a chance to sway the ear of his peers who may be sympathetic to his plight. To have the district court hear a tax case, the taxpayer must pay the tax deficiency and file an administrative claim for a refund. Upon denial of the claim or prolonged administrative inaction, the taxpayer may file a suit in the district court for the refund. The same procedure must be followed if he is simply asserting that he overpaid his taxes. District Court decisions may be appealed to the Court of Appeals.

-- *Court of Claims* is the third avenue which a taxpayer may take to dispute tax assessments made by the IRS. Again the taxpayer must pay the assessment before going to court. The Court of Claims decision is rendered by a judge without the benefit of a jury. A Court of Claims case is heard by a trial judge who renders a report. Usually after further pleadings and oral arguments, the Court of Claims makes its decision largely on the trial judge's report. Court of Claims decisions are final unless the Supreme Court grants certiorari, an unlikely event in tax cases.

-- *Court of Appeals* hears appeals from either the tax court or the district court. The Court of Appeals does not decide factual decisions, only legal principles and their applications to specific cases. It is not uncommon for the eleven circuits to differ on the application of some rules or tax principles. This disturbs the IRS especially when the rules are not applied in favor of the government. It is not uncommon for the IRS to appeal the same principle to several jurisdictions until it receives the decision it wants. Court of Appeals' decisions may be appealed to the Supreme Court.

-- *Supreme Court* rarely hears tax cases. The justices prefer to leave those decisions to lower courts. Since the historic ruling in 1895 which ruled the income tax unconstitutional (remedied by the sixteenth amendment), the highest court has left most taxation questions to the lower courts and the legislature. Constitutional questions on the tax and the application of procedures relating to the collection and levying of the tax have also been settled. Both the due process and self-incrimination questions have been resolved to a greater extent.

If a tax is so arbitrary or capricious as to amount to confiscation, then there is a chance the Supreme Court may consider it. But filing a tax return does not violate the Fifth Amendment privilege against self-incrimination. Without new legislative action, no new Supreme Court decisions can be expected.

AVOIDING AUDITS

The best way to avoid income taxes is never to file a return or to obtain a social security number. This is not only impractical but unrealistic for most people. While certain members of organized crime, prostitutes and drug dealers find it the best way to stay off the IRS list, it precludes any honest employment. However, the majority of underground players are ordinary taxpayers.

The government has developed a method, Estimated Personal Wealth, to nail these professional criminals. Used effectively against Al Capone and recent drug dealers, the IRS investigates the style of life including automobiles, homes, clothes, restaurant bills and even garbage. Then the IRS projects how much money is necessary to support such habits and assesses the appropriate tax. This method has been upheld by the courts. Notoriety or a police investigation is generally needed to trigger this type of investigation.

For the ordinary business person who skims from his business, underreports his income and engages in the full range of underground economic activities, the double set of books have proven reliable since the tax man arrived. The system is remarkably simple but extremely time consuming. The business owner must keep a full set of records which show a reduction in his income, therefore his taxes. Errors in the duplicate set of books will cause an audit and reveal the level and amount of duplicity. But a restaurant owner in San Gabriel who has been audited three times feels comfortable with the audit. His solution, once his duplicate set of books was established, is to increase slightly his income each year and try a "normal" amount of cheating. The IRS always disallows some of his deductions, increases his taxes, but they haven't discovered the true extent of his cheating.

As strange as it may seem, a taxpayer, especially a small business, that is not cheating is more suspicious than someone who is cheating.
Large deductions of any type are likely to attract the IRS computer's attention. Even though the deduction is justified, a human may come by to verify the deduction. Such is the way the system performs.
For the large masses of non-reporters in the "straight time" or "skilled" categories, audits and investigation are avoided by frequent changes in address. Since this group has a small return in dollars considering the expense of finding the person, the IRS lets the account slide as "unable to locate."

This group often, when found, actually may be entitled to a refund. Or they may not be required to file a return for that tax year. The third possibility is the person has died. In any case, the lower the income tax bracket the taxpayer is in, the less his chances for being audited. The purpose of the audit is to collect as much money as possible. Poor people don't have the income to make the IRS want to spend time looking for them.
EVER EXPANDING RULES

The IRS is constantly under pressure to collect more money for the government. The budget deficit is now at $1.3 trillion, the total national debt exceeds $14 trillion, and interest on the national debt is the third largest budget item. The Internal Revenue Service must be a hard nose to collect further taxes. In two specific areas, business and family, the agency is trying to eliminate any income gain.

-- *Family* - Tax rules against dealings within families have been long established. Primarily passed to prevent a family from writing off capital gains or losses in the transfer of property between blood relatives, the IRS has succeeded in pursuing an "anti-family" policy to some extraordinary lengths.

While anyone can make money from his family, no one can lose money on them. The situation as far as the government is concerned is "Heads I win, tails you lose." Congress has approved this arrangement to prevent a father from selling a piece of land to his son for below market value and deducting the loss from his income tax. But the IRS has strictly interpreted this rule to force the taxpayer to be "greedy" with all family members.

If you want to lend money to your son to buy a house, say $50,000 for a down payment, and the IRS audits you, it may charge you a penalty because you did not charge interest on the loan. Why? Because if you left the money in a bank, you would have received interest, which would have been taxable. This way the IRS feels the government has been cheated out of money.

Taking this rule even further, the IRS is implementing a rule which would ban deductions for depreciation or maintenance if you rent property to a relative. This rule would force taxpayers to rent houses to total strangers rather than to relatives because the government says so. Being greedy with relatives is the only situation the IRS will accept. And the common belief that "charity begins at home" is nothing the government cares to recognize.

-- *Business* - Every business tries to arrange its affairs to pay the least amount of taxes legally permissible. Naturally, the IRS doesn't like that situation. Rather, they would have every business pay the maximum tax possible. These mutually exclusive positions have led to a new set of rulings by the IRS which in effect, forces business to rat on itself.

In its audits of corporate tax returns the IRS has been demanding confidential corporate information. Uncooperative companies are immediately assessed a *5percent* negligence penalty. Specifically, the agents are demanding "accrual papers" which forecast debatable tax issues and recommend a certain amount of cash be set aside for possible payment.

By obtaining the confidential memos between the tax advisor and the chief executive officer, the IRS has a map to which deductions the company think might be questionable. The agency will immediately disallow the deduction. A major company can spend $500,000 or more in litigation and accounting costs to fight the IRS invasion. Since the IRS has the broad power to see all relevant materials in a tax audit, the question of these confidential memos has yet to be decided.

To eliminate these papers puts the company in a bind between the IRS and the SEC which requires such tax planning information for investors. The IRS is looking for the easy way to collect more taxes, Since the burden of proof is on the taxpayer to show he is entitled to the deduction, the denial of all grey area deductions would force the company to accept; huge legal bills or to pay the IRS assessment.

By destroying any vestige of corporate privacy, the IRS will simply force corporate officers into more subterfuge and evasive behavior. They will use more convoluted routes to arrive at simple answers. This dangerous attitude can only lead to more evasion rather than compliance with the law.

X

Life, Liberty and the Pursuit of Happiness

"We hold these truths to be self—evident, that all men are created equal, that they are endowed by their Creator with certain unalienable Rights that among these are Life, Liberty, and the Pursuit of Happiness."

Declaration of Independence

Seething just under the surface politic in America is a massive rebellion against taxation and government spending unparalleled in our history since the American Revolution. It has surfaced in the current Tea Party movement as well as in numerous other local revolts against the high cost of government. But beneath a surface calm, underground, more and more people are turning to the belief that politicians are bleeding them to a slow, painful death. A debased currency, inflation and taxation on constructive work strengthen this belief. The common person is falling farther behind as government gobbles up more of the economic pie.

When the income tax was first instituted, it was seen as a way to make the rich pay their fair share of the cost of government. When it became mass tax, it was for the salvation of America and the free world. Now taxes are for the consumption of the insatiable government entities with little regard for the people producing the goods and service. This spending, inflation and a tax system which penalizes work have made the underground economy flourish. The irony is that most American would rather support their government but they must be convinced they are getting a fair deal.

INFLATION

The fastest way to destroy a political system is to destroy its currency. Weimar Germany learned the painful lesson of rampant inflation in the 1920's which directly led to the rise of the Nazi government.

Throughout history, the confidence of a people rests in their economic means of exchange, the coin of the realm.

Throughout most of American history, the central government has stood firmly on the side of a solid dollar. The issuance of the Continental Dollar (not worth a continental) was a catastrophe for the country because the people realized that it was not backed by anything real other than a government promise. The Federal government of the United States began issuing currency which was backed by a solid commodity, generally gold. In fact, the United States defended the gold standard at $32 an ounce from 1932 until 1969.

Since floating the value of dollar, the purchasing power of the dollar has been in precipitous decline. As in countries with chronic inflation like Zimbabwe, Americans have learned an economic reality which runs counter to their personal morality. Until recent years, the economic morality paid off for the average person. Working, saving and living within our means meant economic success and well-being for the present as well as the future. Inflation destroys our cherished rules while substituting a series of conflicting values.

Inflation creates a conflict between economic interests of the individual and the society as a whole. While thrift, frugality, work and investment in the future were the backbone of our economic vitality, this new set of economic rules have debased even our philosophical outlook. Deficit spending learned from the government and encouraged by the banking community has become the way of life. Use today, pay tomorrow because tomorrow the same object will cost more and the dollar will be worth less. Mortgaging the future seems to be a way of life among American politicians. And this living on the backs of the next generation is breaking down the good sense economic order. The recent banking crisis was fueled by an excessive of borrowing for real estate on the assumption that the underlying asset would forever increase in value.

Inflation has a profound direct effect on the taxes paid by Americans. While the notion of graduated income tax is excellent in theory, inflation ruins the reality of it. Tax rate bracket creep continues to drive people into higher tax categories. The dreaded Alternative

Minimum Income tax (AMT) was never indexed for inflation and each year can ensnare millions of people. To avoid its reach, the taxpayer is dependent upon Congress to temporarily increase its limits each year rather than fixing the problem once and for all by indexing it.

The 2010 dollar is worth only 36 cents in 1980 dollars. This depreciation of the primary value of currency has led to a call for a return to the gold standard or some basket of commodities because monetary authorities cannot control spending by political interests. The drawback is that there isn't enough yellow metal to adequately back all of the dollars in existence. That was the compelling reason given for going to a floating rate of exchange.

Inflation also reduces the value of any capital which citizens manage to save over a period of time. Liquid cash in savings accounts or savings bonds which currently paid next to nothing are economic suicide if rampant inflation begins again. The hardest hit, of course, is the small unsophisticated investor, the little guy who tries to put a few dollars away from each paycheck in a savings account. The slower he saves the less the savings is worth when he goes to spend it. This causes more people to save less money.

THE ENDLESS SPENDING SPREE

Most Americans run a sound house where money isn't spent until it is earned. The old American adages "Waste not, want not" and "A penny saved is a penny earned" have not penetrated the major maker of inflation, the Federal government. Since the inception of the income tax, but more specifically since its transformation into a mass tax in 1942, government spending has increased to astronomical levels.

Spending alone isn't the cause of citizens' cynicism, rather the waste, fraud and constant deficits which run contrary to good sense have hardened Americans attitudes toward paying taxes. By adopting the Keynesian notion that all recessions are caused by a lack of demand, the government has been consuming a larger and larger percentage of goods and services in the American economy even though the government does not have the tax revenue to pay for those goods.

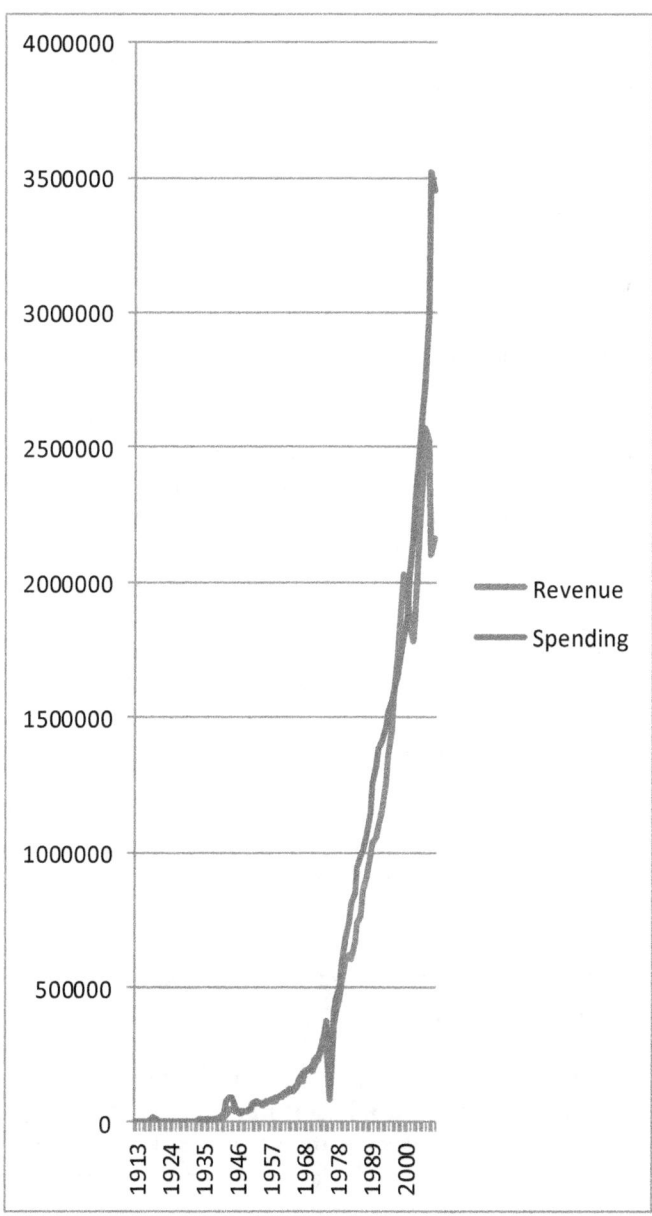

Figure 4 - Federal Revenue vs. Spending 1913-2010

Social engineering is the password for the massive deficits which the government regularly runs. Politicians can justify every dollar of "your" money they spend on "their" priorities.

Our government depends on the amount of money it can extract from its citizens. And as the most expensive government ever devised by human mind, dollars are spent in the abstract. Government officials, by their nature, will never spend the money wisely because the wealth seems endless. Money is like water, if you must draw it from a well and carry it on your back, you use it more wisely than if you only have to turn on a tap.

In 25 of the last 30 years the government has spent more than it has collected in taxes. In order to meet obligations, the Federal government is borrowing nearly $1 trillion a year which has pushed the national debt to nearly $14 trillion, that is a debt of $30,000 for every American. In 1940, the per capita debt was only $325. 23. The reckless spending has pushed the interest payments on the debt to $400 billion a year, the largest expenditure in the Federal budget after social security, medicine, human services and defense. This massive borrowing in the private credit markets has soaked up the available money for plant expansion, home mortgages, car loans and other necessary consumer and business borrowing.

The bureaucracy of government has a vested interest in inefficiency and size protecting its minions and the well-organized lobbying groups lined up for government handouts. In addition the public sector unions have run up staggering pension obligations that must be paid by all individual tax payers. And government has become the victim of its own size, inattentive to detail, forgetful and unable to police the billions of dollars it spends.

Without private sector controls like profit and loss, personal motivation and market demand, government provides goods and service without regard to cost or market needs. Programs are only considered successful if they grow larger. And no program ever ends even when times change, like the beekeeper indemnity program or the National Board for the Promotion of Rifle Practice.

The wasteful, unnecessary and other extraneous programs have changed the relationship between state and citizen. Government is a contract among people for mutual protection against foreign and domestic threats and to provide basic human needs of food, clothing and shelter. Once those terms of the social contract are fulfilled, government engages in economic redistribution, special interest manipulation (fleecing the taxpayers) and social engineering.

While social goals may be ideal in theory, government implementation of these programs has proved to be a rousing failure. From the New Deal's Social Security system to Great Society spending programs, Congressional spending has failed to solve social problems. But a great many white collar professionals have gained employment and government contracts in the process. Taxes which are levied to pay for these programs are succeeding in slowing the real growth of the economy and damaging the opportunity of all Americans for a better life. High tax rates have reduced incentive and boosted the membership in the underground economy.

All government entities are overhead that is placed upon private businesses and citizens. It is a question that the citizenry must answer - how much government do we need to pay for to get the job done?

In the 18th Century, English economist Adam Smith wrote, "high taxes, sometimes by diminishing consumption of the taxed commodities and sometimes by encouraging smuggling, afford smaller revenue to government than what might be drawn from more moderate taxes." Great Britain built the world's largest empire on these laisse-faire ideas. The 19th Century United States followed the same line of prosperity, passing Great Britain as the world's largest economy after the First World War.

That war was the changing point in history because it was the first time governments took total control of their economies for the war effort. The Great Depression and the Second World War established big government as a fixture in America. The income tax made the government flush with cash and politicians able to richly reward their supporters.

John Maynard Keynes enunciated an economic theory in the 1920's which has become the gospel of Western governments ever since. His theory contended that a lack of demand caused economic downturns and it was the duty of government to stimulate demand by spending to "prime the pump" of the economy. While this mixture of Bloomsbury elitism and deficit spending did not end the depression (World War II did), it provided the theoretical framework for government to have a limitless purse and justification to dabble in governmental social engineering.

When the Roosevelt administration brought the social elite into government, it provided the Washington bureaucracy with a cloak of righteousness and correctness. The central government began believing that wisdom could only be found along the banks of the Potomac. And special interests, hungry for that tax dollar converged on the city, seeking a piece of the pie.

With the professional economist moving into the government, endless attempts at "fine tuning" the economy have been attempted. The dismal failure rate of this planned economy approach is evident to all policy makers. The great financial collapse of 2008 was brought about as much by government entities of Fannie Mae and Freddie Mac backing fraudulent mortgages as it was by the financial manipulation of Wall Street.

Inflation is a product of the government demand which Keynes thought was too small. The social welfare states of Europe are suffering from the same excess of government consumption. Keynes theory can only work when government is not the profligate spender during normal times. When the inevitable downturn comes, governments cannot continue to borrow to continue spending at even increased levels. The huge disconnect with today's politicians is they do not understand that prior to the great depression; governments only spent the revenue they raised. Increasing government spending during a downturn in the economy was to be only "temporary." Government should resume its normal function of only spend the revenue it has collected when the emergency ends.

Tax evasion is a worldwide phenomenon proving that the theory of socialism is not compatible with the basic nature of human beings.

Sweden, once one of the purest welfare states, was almost bankrupt from the unbridled growth of government and the decline in individual productivity. The government finally had to rein in programs and encourage productive behavior in the private sector. The social welfare state, as an idea, has immense appeal; human laziness and stifling bureaucracy destroy the idea when applied to a national economy. Government is unable to restrain spending or to impose self-discipline upon its own consumption habits.

TAXING AWAY INCENTIVE

Taxes have become significant factors when many economic transactions take place. Thinking tax consequences first, economic effect second, makes for poor business and personal use of capital. With taxes growing faster than inflation or personal income, incentive is on the side of the tax avoider.

In the past 15 years, government has been the fastest rising cost in our economic system. Federal, state and local taxes along with social security, unemployment and other transfer payments can total nearly 50percent of income. Earning an additional dollar makes more sense underground than in the legitimate economy.

Double taxation cuts deeper into the dutiful individual who saves money or invests it in the stock of productive corporations. The tax on savings interest makes spending money wiser than saving it. The marginal tax rate discourages individuals from seeking additional work, and then discourages them from saving what he earns. It becomes more profitable to hide the additional dollars of earning than to declare them.

This marginal tax rate has been accentuated over the past few years as the value of the dollar has eroded while pushing individuals into higher tax brackets thus cheapening the value of deductions. "Bracket creep" will tax away nearly $45 billion from individual incomes this year. Individuals or families who are trying to keep pace with economic uncertainly find the more they earn, the larger the tax bite and the lower the real income.

123

If you prudently invested $10,000 five years ago in real estate and you sell the land today for $15,000 you show a gain of $5,000. But if the rate of inflation had averaged 10 percent for each of the past five years, your real gain is actually a loss. What you've done is almost stay even with the rate of inflation. Now enter the government who sees that $5000 as capital gains and takes 20 percent of it after five years of investment, you actually lose money because of combined inflation and taxation. This formula is repeated for businesses as well resulting in a net transfer of capital to government and away from the private sector.

Naturally, the IRS does not like to deal in "real dollars" when computing tax rates. This would force the government to decide in favor of the public on most tax questions. It would also reduce the "inflation tax" which politicians favor.

Tax cut talk, which usually accompanies elections, has never been a real tax cut. Since the inception of the income tax, tax revenue has never decreased but tax rates have been, from time to time, readjusted to give the image of change. In the real economic world, a tax cut in 2002 is not going to offset the increase in social security and Medicare tax and inflation costs of fuel, food and other items. What actually happens, if it happens, is that the government increases its tax take and gives back as a "favor" to the electorate a small amount making it a net increase for the year. This still translates into more for the government, less for the individual that once again fuels tax evasion. Or as American humorist Peg Bracken observed, "Why does a slight tax increase cost me two hundred dollars and a substantial tax cut save me thirty cents?"

Over the past 80 years, inflation has been a constant in every economic system. Politically, this allows Congress to pass periodic tax cuts in attempts to curry the favor of the electorate who is paying the bills. Indexing the income tax to the Consumer Price Index or some other measure of inflation would deprive politicians of the illusionary game of tax cuts. It would also decrease real government revenue while reducing the distortion tax rates now have on the economic system. Keeping inflation under control and a strong dollar would be much more important to all politicians.

Supply side economists like Laffer, Roberts and Mundeli argue forcefully on the need to cut "real" tax rates especially on business investment and individual tax rates. By using classical economic theory, these economists cite the failures of government at "fine tuning" the economy and recommend a longer range policy focused on growth of the private sector and tax policy to encourage capital investment and individual savings.

While these theories sound noble on paper, they have yet to be converted into economic policy with the accompanying political modifications which may cause them to go awry. Larger government deficits, more inflation and a faster bracket creep would drive more not less people into the underground economy. Capital in the form of cash, piles up unproductively in safe deposit boxes rather than in savings accounts. And another noble theory will bite the dust. Strong politicians with extraordinary foresight will be needed to carry through supply-side policies and it remains to be seen if such men and women occupy our elected offices. The new economic realities of massive deficits will force all government officials to cut government spending and create a new economic policy based upon fiscal sanity and common sense.

FINANCIAL POLICE

While there is a desire for equality among Americans, there is an even more fundamental desire for freedom from government. The unique quality about the American way of life is freedom of choice and the other guarantees in the Bill of Rights. When that document was written, the Founding Fathers did not foresee the Internal Revenue Service.

Over the years, technology has begun to catch up with the Orwellian concept of Big Brother who monitors all the movements of every citizen. The advent of the high speed computer, advanced databases and economic reporting software has made the novel *1984* literally possible. The IRS now has the capacity in hardware to cross-check every tax return of every individual in the country. It also has files on bank accounts, investments, land, family, occupation, number of times married, as well as a road map to every place, job, and major transaction you have performed in your life. In fact, with the advent of electronic filing, the IRS district offices and the central one in West Virginia hold more information on the citizens of this nation than any other file of any other government which ever existed on the face of the earth.

This vast amount of information is limited by time, manpower and money. The IRS, like all other government agencies, insists that if it had more money, it could do a more effective job of collecting taxes. The underground economy is the segment which is most often discussed before Congressional committees. Statements that the Federal deficit would be wiped out if the underground economy was taxed fail to take notice of the lack of personal freedom or the massive intrusion of tax agents into every aspect of daily life. Nor does it take into account the amount of work that will no longer be worth doing.

To blunt criticism that the agency wasn't doing enough to combat the underground dollar, IRS agents have taken to raiding restaurants, examining cash register receipts and assessing those sneaky waitresses and bartenders for a year's worth of taxes. From the Mom and Pop grocery stores, small corporations and other minor figures in the tax avoidance scheme have also felt the vengeful pen of the auditor because, as the agency thinks, they have neither the legal clout nor accounting sophistication to wage a winning battle against the agency. The IRS picks its fights to win.

While celebrities will always be a target for the tax audit because of the free publicity they give the agency, the natural extension of that bias selection was the Nixon "enemies list." In using the agency to harass political opponents and groups, Nixon opened the Pandora's Box of totalitarian control. While Congressional laws and assurance were passed to prevent this particular series of events from happening again, any law can be circumscribed. Just look at the tax laws and tax shelters. And when politicians and members of Congress begin referring to the opposition party as "enemies," strict controls and limits on the government are even more important.

The complexity of the tax laws also provides the IRS with pretext to investigate any citizen at any time. There is no reasonable or probable cause requirement imposed on the agency. Conceivably, a citizen could be approached by a tax agent on the street and be forced into an immediate audit. (The agency prefers to do this at home or at a place of business.)

The particular anti-family bias of the tax laws is making a profound impact on the social fabric of the country. If relatives cannot loan money, rent houses, conduct business or sell assets to loved and trusted family members without an IRS investigation, the basic unit of our society is in deep trouble. While the rules were written to prevent the "very rich" from concealing their wealth, (a dubious concept to begin with) the rules are now preventing parents from converting their upstairs rooms to an apartment for their newlywed children who can't afford a house because of high unemployment and taxes. The IRS would prefer you to put your elderly parents in nursing homes rather than keep them in your house because it makes the accounting procedures neater.

Giving gifts to parents on social security is taxable after the first $3000, a ridiculously low number considering the value of that money in "real" terms. It is the same for parents loaning money to children starting out and needing money to begin a home. While the standard gifting of $11,000 annual per parent per child exists, carefully planning is necessary to help them along. The standard answer in these cases from the IRS is "It's the law." This misleading statement doesn't mention that it is really the IRS's interpretation of its own rules which makes the law. Or, how can the agency collect the maximum tax from any law written while permitting the least advantage to the taxpayer? "Reasonable" is not in the IRS lexicon of audit terms. "Average, Standard, Approved"- they make it, but there is no reasonable or liveable standard applied to taxation.

RETURNING TO THE FOLD

With $1 trillion dollars in the Underground Economy, it would be in the best interest to all Americans to return some part of that to the legitimate economy. But that decision is both political and psychological in nature. While NEW economic policies may help in preventing more defections or increased use of the cash economy, nothing short of a major overhaul of the income tax code will restore confidence in the system.

As mentioned earlier, the tax system was accepted as a way to offset declining Federal revenues from import tariffs, excise taxes and the sale of government lands. But the two World Wars, the depression and the acceptance of a modified welfare state increased the cost of government to the incomprehensible levels of today. The tax system expanded from those who could afford pay to everyone who worked in the name of equality. But the rules in only 90 years have become too complicated for an educated person to understand, and inflation has pushed moderate incomes into higher tax brackets.

The tax system, used as a method of social engineering encourages spending, discourages savings and forces evasion. Expanding the definition of taxable income insures that no thinking person can or would comply with the filing requirements. Taxing the lowest incomes, where people are barely getting by, forces errors on the system because of little education. The scope and complexity of the income tax system assures the government that a sizeable underground economy will exist. But there are steps, many which would require unheard of political courage that could bring segments of the underground economy to the surface.

-- *Tax Bracket Indexing* – When the average taxpayer loses ground to inflation, the increased tax demand on salaries is resented as unfair. The inflation tax undermines faith in our tax system. By indexing the tax brackets to the annual rate of inflation or the Consumer Price Index would allow the individual to keep at least the same percentage of his wages each year. Inflation wage increases would not be taxed away leaving us poorer with each salary increase. Politically possible, the major drawback is that the Federal government would lose the "easy way" to take more money from individual wage earners. The incentive for government to retard inflation would become a matter of self-interest. Such action might balance to the tax consumption of the state with the earning power of the individual making personal and corporate planning "more efficient."

-- *Eliminate Double Taxation* – Both savings and dividends are taxed twice. Our low rate of savings is due to both our profligate nature and the taxation of saved money. To encourage capital formation, the Federal government must remove saving account interest and corporate dividends from the double taxation. The reason savings are taxed was the government belief during the depression that saving money equaled "hoarding", a behavior that needed to be punished. So by taxing the savings of the citizen, the government would encourage spending. And this spending would be good for the economy but not necessarily the individual. By doing so, many of the tax shelter gimmicks that do not produce valuable production will be eliminated. Money for housing, plant expansion, new machinery and modernization would become available at a lower cost. Chrysler, General Motors and numerous other businesses could again rely on the private credit markets rather than government guaranteed loans.

The vaguely socialist notion that the rich would benefit at the expense of the poor is nonsense. Present policy is depriving the entire nation of the necessary capital for investment in the future. Small investors with limited sophistication will be helped by such a measure since they are more likely to keep money in savings accounts, CD's and simple mutual funds. Again, the objection on the part of Washington is that it will "cost the government money" meaning cut into the money politicians have to spend. Adequate political compromises can be reached with a little fortitude from our legislators. Money will remain in a liquid usable form rather than be locked away in collectibles like gold, silver; art, antiques and other collectibles.

-- *"Reasonable and Prudent Man Rule"* – While the IRS has every reason to believe that people cheat on their taxes, considering the complexity of the tax codes, the ineptitude of commercial preparers and the guilty until proven innocent rule of tax law, the taxpayer has good reason to hate and avoid the IRS. By enforcing a consistency rule on the agency, taxpayers can be assured that a tax case's disposition will not depend on the tax court. Also if a tax case goes to court with the taxpayer winning, the IRS should be required to pay all court and attorney's fees. This might cut down on the IRS's willingness to litigate a taxpayer into submission. Another possibility is to make any advice given to a taxpayer by IRS employees binding on the agency. Taxpayers could then ask the IRS field offices for advice and feel certain that the correct procedure was being followed.

The present system of permitting *ex post facto* decisions by the IRS is unfair to every taxpayer. These proposals would run into serious opposition from the IRS and its friends on Capitol Hill. But they would be viewed as fair play by the American people. A recent proposal by a Congressman would require all members of Congress to prepare their own Tax Returns without professional advice. Of course, the proposal will go nowhere but if adopted the tax code would quickly become simpler.

-- *Taxing Marijuana* – With nearly $48 billion dollars in sales each year, the pot industry is totally out of control of the government. Various proposals to place marijuana in the same category as alcohol and tobacco (both hazardous substances) have received little consideration in the past because of the political climate. But the billions in tax revenue could be collected by the government in a similar manner as now used with both of these other substances. Without judging the morality of the issue, the economic argument for legalization and taxation are as compelling as the repeal of the 18th Amendment was in 1933. The present system is not working. Bringing this economic transaction out of the subterranean twilight into the legitimate business world would make it easier to control and monitor while providing a major new source of revenue for the government.

The recent budget debacles in California and other places have given new credence to the discussion of taxing an outlawed substance. With medical marijuana laws already on the books in 11 states, the discussion about the forbidden weed is actually getting debated in a more rational matter. Proposition 19 in 2010 in California actually proposed to legalize the possession and cultivation of pot for the first time in a century. Proponents suggest that a legalized and taxed pot industry in California would raise $1.4 billion in new taxes. While still in conflict with Federal laws, the decriminalization at the local level would create the tax windfall that may make the legalization to irresistible to a large number of states.

-- *Value Added Tax* – Adopted in many European countries, this glorified sales tax is an effort to tax consumption rather than production. Its major problems are: it has become an additional tax rather than a replacement tax, therefore increasing the overall tax rate; it is manipulated by political and economic interest thus becoming as confusing as conventional tax systems; and it bears heaviest on the poorest segments of the population because it is a sales tax. The VAT has been discussed in Congress but little enthusiasm or support was found. If coupled with a proportional reduction in income and corporate taxes, the VAT could be an effective measure to tax consumption of wealth not its production.

However, the European experience is a cautionary tale about opening a door to a new tax with the politicians assuring the public that the tax will only apply to a certain level of society or it will be placed at a very modest rate. While voters in Europe were promised VAT's of only 4percent when they were being asked to approve it, today the VAT is from 17-21percent depending upon the country. The voters were not asked if they wanted to increase the tax rate. If the country were ever to adopt a VAT, it would be very important that a supermajority provision is put in place to allow any increase to it. I would prefer a three quarters majority but two thirds would be acceptable.

-- *Flat Tax* – A flat tax has been advanced many times by a variety of politicians. In reality, it is simple a return to the original idea of the income tax as proposed and passed as the 16th amendment. No matter what the source of income, it is taxed at one rate. Deductions would be eliminated so no favored party such as farmers, homeowners, gas and oil companies who due to effective lobbying efforts would pay less. Significant proposal that would allow a large base exemption (like the original income tax) would continue to make the tax fair. Proposals suggesting $26,000 as the base exemption have been proposed. More detailed proposals from Hall-Rabushka have been advanced but not as serious congressional proposals. A big drawback to a flat tax is that it would eliminate a major fund-raising tool for politicians – doing a favor in the tax code for a campaign contribution. The key element in its favor, however, is simplicity to understand and enforce. Something that is rarely discussed it that the current Alternative Minimum Tax (ATM) is very close to a flat tax because it eliminates most deductions. All of the arguments against the flat tax tend to focus on the issue of a graduated tax. A flat tax approach that eliminates deductions treats all income the same, and has a graduated level based upon absolute dollars indexed for inflation would significantly simply the current tax code while addressing the issues of the rich paying fewer taxes based upon their source of income (dividends and capital gains.) A simple formula of zero tax on the first $60,000; 10percent tax on the next $100,000; 15percent on the next $200,000 and 20percent on income over $360,000 might put a great many accountants and tax lawyers out of business.

The flat tax would be very progressive with those who make more, pay more. And it would eliminate the distortion of how the money is made (wage, dividend, capital gain) because it would be taxed based upon your total income. Without resorting to class warfare rhetoric, everyone can again aspire to be in the top tax category based upon the fundamental principles that has made America great.

THE IMPOSSIBLE DREAM

A perfectly equitable tax system coupled with a prudent and frugal government is the ideal situation which will never be achieved. Though Marxist theory and Jeffersonian democracy conceive of such a situation on paper, experience has taught differently. Governments grow according to their ability to collect taxes from its people. (This was evident in the Soviet Union, Bourbon France, the Roman Empire and the United States.) Every industrial nation of the world has an underground economy which flourishes because of the demand of the population rather than government fiat. In Germany, it is known as "schwarzarbeit." France calls off the books work, "travail noir," while Italy calls it "black labor." Britain calls it "the fiddle" and Argentina calls it "morocho."

The desire of government officials who see payroll deductions as the only efficient way of collecting taxes are constantly angered over the numbers who avoid taxes. But any crusades to stop underground money will fail. They failed in the highly organized Soviet police state. Individuals will take risks for appropriate economic gains.

Properly, government should try to encourage legal participation in the economy. Cash is an inefficient use of a nation's resources except when the government is intruding on every economic activity. Bank filing requirements for any transaction over $5000 is a reason not to use a bank - for privacy reasons as much as for any illegal reason.

Moralists pass laws, like prohibition or pot laws, that drive entire industries into the cash economy. These activities cost money to the economy without producing the desired suppression of the activity. These economic crimes of buying and selling forbidden products also produce violent crime. If they were legalized and taxed, the cost of law enforcement would also decline.

Today, the sentiment in the country runs against the big government model that taxes and spends. It is seen as the largest single source of waste in the country. The government produces few goods and service yet taxes devour over 35 percent of the average paycheck.

The amount of information entrusted to the government is suspect based upon the enormous power of advanced computers. Where once the amount of information fed into the system worked in favor of the individual because the volume was too great for the system to process, now it becomes a dossier on each citizen's life. The central government will soon be able to synthesize a composite picture of any individual through its computer files. While privacy advocates voice concern about Google and other private companies, the government has created a huge system out of the view of any private citizen.

While the ideal mix between individual responsibility to support government and government restraint in intruding into the private affairs of its citizens has yet to be reached, the constant shifting of position must swing back to favor the individual. For 80 years, we have experienced a massive centralization of power. The underground economy is not strictly a reaction to this governmentalization of life. The dragnet of rules and regulations has included the previously excluded activities of our society. The income tax has strayed from its original intent to augment government revenues by taxing those with sufficient income to afford it.

For the first time in our history, we are aware of too much government in our lives. As our revolutionary forbearers knew, government is a social contract among the governed. When large segments of the population are excluded from that process, or feel alienated from it, the resulting rules are the products of organized special interests. Consensus politics produce the most prosperous society.

Unchecked government growth is a massive overhead cost that all the productive elements of society must support. The question is how heavy of a weight can we bear – and how much of it is necessary? Government consumption of wealth clogs the economic river of our country like the hyacinth, beautiful on the surface but whose tangled roots suffocate the movement of life. Soon the river becomes a stagnant swamp and the economy becomes a neglected backwater rather than the life blood of the world. China, India, Brazil and other countries are looking to dethrone America as the world's premier economic power. How ironic that "communist" China is often more interested in the success of its businesses to grow and prosper than "capitalist" America.

The United States is still the beacon to the world offering economic opportunity. It is the place people come to work and succeed. The politicians of this country should be loudly applauding and encouraging the risk taking entrepreneurs and working feverishly to remove obstacles to their success. The success of the American private sector provides for the opportunity, prosperity and peace of the citizens of this great country.

www.ingramcontent.com/pod-product-compliance
Lightning Source LLC
Chambersburg PA
CBHW070144290526
45789CB00002B/617